The Greatest 100 Albums To Own On Vinyl

© SONA BOOKS Ltd 2019

CAT NO: SON0440

ISBN: 978-1-912918-05-8

First published in the UK 2019 by Sona Books an imprint of Danann Publishing Ltd.

Copy Editor Juliette O'Neill

THE GREATEST

ALBUMS
TO OWN ON VINYL

The must have records for your collection

sona
BOOKS

Welcome to The Greatest 100 Albums To Own On Vinyl

In *The Greatest 100 Albums To Own On Vinyl*, we collate the greatest albums to have ever been pressed and then sold on vinyl since the '50s. From the bands and solo artists that made the music possible, to the sleeve art and limited edition extras of the record itself, we will take you on the ultimate journey of musical discovery.

Contents

'50s-60s

In The Wee Small Hours

Frank Sinatra

Release Date: 1955 | Record Label: Capitol

Pushing 40 years old in April 1955 and already nine albums into an uneven career, Frank Sinatra needed his third record for the Capitol label to be a major hit — and so it was, but almost uniquely for Sinatra, not solely because of his vocal prowess or the quality of the songs. *In The Wee Small Hours* is a resolutely downbeat collection of songs which focus on solitude, abandonment and inner reflection — a long way from the cheerful, optimistic pop-swing in which Sinatra had previously specialised — and as such was something of a commercial gamble in the popular music market of the mid-'50s.

This was Sinarta's ninth album and his third with Capitol

A large part of the album's success (it went all the way to #2 on the American chart) is attributable to its fantastic cover, which alone makes it worth your while acquiring it on vinyl. Lit with blue light and resolutely lonesome, Sinatra is pictured in a desolate cityscape with nothing but a cigarette for company. Nowadays, film noir and bleak televisual hits such as *Mad Men* have made us accustomed to the image of the so-lonely-he's-cool suited man, but back in '55, this kind of understated chic was new to most of the mass audience. Hats off to Sinatra, then, who had been pondering the concept for at least a decade before the album was recorded.

Of course, it helped that many of the songs on the LP — Sinatra's first 12" vinyl release, and the first of its kind outside the classical and jazz fields — were first-rate. The title cut and *'Glad To Be Unhappy'* presented the singer as a man bowed but unbroken by his solitude, while I *'Get Along Without You Very Well'* — with its luscious orchestration, arranged by the masterful Nelson Riddle — is quite possibly one of the most accomplished post-breakup songs ever written.

These immortal compositions, many of them now part and parcel of the *Great American Songbook*, paved the way for what was perhaps Sinatra's finest album — *Songs For Swingin' Lovers!*, released the following year.

Track List

SIDE A

Track 1: In The Wee Small Hours Of The Morning
Track 2: Mood Indigo
Track 3: Glad To Be Unhappy
Track 4: I Get Along Without You Very Well
Track 5: Deep In A Dream
Track 6: I See Your Face Before Me
Track 7: Can't We Be Friends?
Track 8: When Your Lover Has Gone

SIDE B

Track 1: What Is This Thing Called Love?
Track 2: Last Night When We Were Young
Track 3: I'll Be Around
Track 4: Ill Wind
Track 5: It Never Entered My Mind
Track 6: Dancing On The Ceiling
Track 7: I'll Never Be The Same
Track 8: This Love Of Mine

ELLA FITZGERALD

Like Someone In Love

Ella Fitzgerald

Release Date: 1957 | **Record Label:** Verve

One of no fewer than four albums released by Ella Fitzgerald in 1957, *Like Someone In Love* is an album of standards — and although the songs may be lesser known than the many other compositions she covered throughout her 'Song book' period, they're no less evocative for that.

Soulful, emotional and sweet, the songs are evoked neatly by Phil Stern's cover photo of Fitzgerald, then 50 years old and peaking as a singer. Caught with an expression of rapture, the singer never seemed more inspired than she does here, especially if you've been wise enough to invest in the full-sized LP artwork.

Fans of this world-class period in Fitzgerald's career will relish the song choices on the album. The title track, composed by veteran tunesmiths in 1944 by Jimmy Van Heusen and Johnny Burke, had been a hit back in 1945 for Bing Crosby; Fitzgerald's reading of the song is both emotional and joyful. Bernice Petkere's *'Close Your Eyes'*, 24 years old at this point, is another high point, with subtle walking bass and a full range of emotive vocals from the singer.

Lionel Hampton's *'Midnight Sun'* features the great Stan Getz on tenor saxophone and has one of Fitzgerald's most considered vocal performances, ranging all the way down to a sultry low that perfectly expresses the late-night vibe of the song. Meanwhile, *'I Thought About You'* showcases her ability to navigate tricky chord changes with consummate ease.

Fitzgerald followed up *Like Someone In Love* with the widely-acclaimed *Porgy And Bess*, recorded with Louis Armstrong, and continued this purple patch of creativity for another decade or so. Disciples of her work might nominate this collection of songs as one of her very finest, thanks to the exquisite arrangements, the purity of her vibrato and the commitment with which she made other songwriters' words sound like her own. Producer Norman Granz, a titan among mid-century jazz studio masters, brought out the very best in Fitzgerald with this exquisite album.

Ella Fitzgerald released four albums in 1957

Track List

SIDE A

Track 1:	There's A Lull In My Life
Track 2:	More Than You Know
Track 3:	What Will I Tell My Heart?
Track 4:	I Never Had A Chance
Track 5:	Close Your Eyes
Track 6:	We'll Be Together Again
Track 7:	Then I'll Be Tired Of You
Track 8:	Like Someone In Love

SIDE B

Track 1:	Midnight Sun
Track 2:	I Thought About You
Track 3:	You're Blasé
Track 4:	Night Wind
Track 5:	What's New?
Track 6:	Hurry Home
Track 7:	How Long Has This Been Going On?

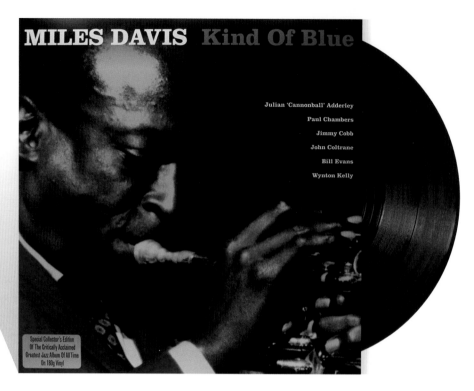

MILES DAVIS Kind Of Blue

Julian 'Cannonball' Adderley
Paul Chambers
Jimmy Cobb
John Coltrane
Bill Evans
Wynton Kelly

Special Collector's Edition Of The Critically Acclaimed Greatest Jazz Album Of All Time On 180g Vinyl

Kind Of Blue

Miles Davis

Release Date: 1959 | **Record Label:** Columbia

One of the things that we love about listening to vinyl is the warmth it offers in terms of its tone and overall sound. That richness is amplified tenfold when listening to a suitable genre like jazz, and it becomes even more essential to the overall experience when feeling the sweet dulcet tones of Miles Davis' trumpet solos in *Kind Of Blue*. It will also make you understand why it is that so many people say that you feel jazz instead of simply listen to it.

There's a reason why *Kind Of Blue* is the best selling jazz album of all time, it's simply unmatched in both its compositions and its tone, delivering a smooth, tantalising sound that feels perfect for almost any occasion. The original 1959 release might only feature five tracks in total, but also required just six takes to record — only the Hispanic-influenced *'Flamenco Sketches'* needed a second take — such was the tightness of the seven-piece band that Davis had formed for his sixth album under Columbia Records.

The cover of *Kind Of Blue* is simple and understated, choosing to focus on Miles as he performs on his iconic trumpet. And yet the liner notes of the LP give a great insight into how he constructed his meticulous-sounding masterpiece, thanks to a series of fascinating notes from pianist Bill Evans linking the improvisation of Davis with a

Japanese visual art style where the artist is forced to be spontaneous. It also explains the difficulty behind group improvisation and how Davis would typically conceive the settings that he required for his pieces mere hours before the actual recording dates.

Jazz might not be for you, but you owe it to yourself to experience a master at the height of his powers and even if you've never appreciated jazz before, *Kind Of Blue* will make you reconsider your stance on it. It's that kind of landmark achievement that deserves to find its way into any vinyl lover's collection.

Track List

SIDE A
Track 1: So What
Track 2: Freddie Freeloader
Track 3: Blue In Green
SIDE B
Track 1: All Blues
Track 2: Flamenco Sketches

Davis performing live on stage in 1970

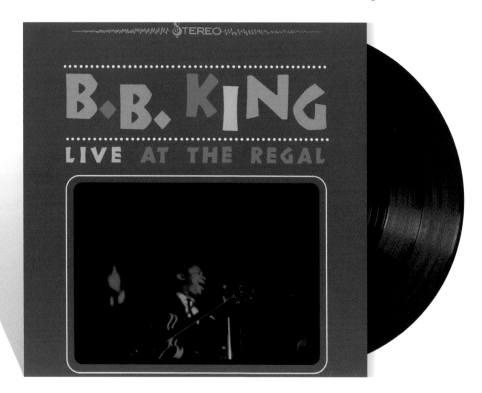

Live At The Regal

BB King

Release Date: 1965 | Record Label: ABC

There's no wonder that the late BB King's 1965 in-concert album *Live At The Regal* was selected a few years back for permanent inclusion in the National Recording Registry at the Library of Congress in Washington, DC. It depicts a bluesman at the peak of his considerable skills, recorded in what was pristine sound quality by the standards of the mid-'60s, playing a set of emotional blues compositions and accompanied by a world-class band. All these years later, it remains an object lesson in electric blues, and has been cited as an inspiration by King disciples such as Eric Clapton.

BB King with his famous guitar Lucille

Around half of the songs on the LP are King's own compositions or co-writes: of these, *'Woke Up This Mornin'* is a particularly dexterous example of King's incredible stage presence. Singing with all of his rich vocal range and delivering plangent solos on his beloved Gibson ES-355, or 'Lucille' as it was known, the great man entranced the audience throughout a series of key and time changes. Elsewhere, King proved his musicianship to a bewildering degree on standards such as Memphis Slim's *'Every Day I Have The Blues'*, powering his way through the song at breakneck speed. Conversely, you coulld settle into the slow grooves of Plumber and Taub's classic *'Worry, Worry'*, on which King supplies an emotive, throat-shredding vocal.

The last of the 'Three Kings' of the blues, predeceased by Freddie King and Albert King, BB was a legend unto himself by the time he died in 2015 at the ripe old age of 89. *Live At The Regal* wasn't his most polished album, because he also released a stunning 40-plus studio LPs, but it was one of his most creative. Audiences loved it and continue to do so, judging by the plethora of reissues which it has enjoyed since it first appeared five decades ago. You should pick up an original mono vinyl for authenticity, although the later stereo versions obviously provide a more in-depth listening experience.

Track List

SIDE A

Track 1:	Every Day I Have the Blues
Track 2:	Sweet Little Angel
Track 3:	It's My Own Fault
Track 4:	How Blue Can You Get
Track 5:	Please Love Me

SIDE B

Track 1:	You Upset Me Baby
Track 2:	Worry, Worry
Track 3:	Woke Up This Mornin'
Track 4:	You Done Lost Your Good Thing Now
Track 5:	Help The Poor

A Love Supreme

John Coltrane

Release Date: 1965 | Record Label: Impulse!

In December 1964 John Coltrane and his Classic Quartet recorded *A Love Supreme* in one session. How many great albums were recorded in a day? A second session was used to record the album with a sextet as this was how Coltrane originally imaged it sounding but he chose to use the quartet version. At 33 minutes, *A Love Supreme* is a four-part suite on Coltrane's spiritual awakening and rebirth from a life of alcohol and drug addiction, with tracked named *'Acknowledgement'*, *'Resolution'*, *'Pursuance'* and *'Psalm'*. But the record in no way preaches

spirituality. It goes from jazz bob to freeform jazz and there is a hint of gospel in there such as when Coltrane repeats the words 'a love supreme' during *'Acknowledgement'*. When the record was released in January 1965 it exceeded all expectations, selling around 500,000 copies. Coltrane's other records would typically sell in the area of 30,000. One of the most influential jazz albums, not only has he influenced those in its own genre, but *A Love Supreme* has been credited with inspiring musicians outside of jazz such as the rock band U2 and guitarist Carlos Santana.

On the album's 50th anniversary a reissue titled the *Complete Masters* was released on vinyl. This version comes with three LPs, in addition to the original album the set includes the only live recording of *A Love Supreme* in its entirety and the third LP has alternative takes, such as the versions recorded in the second session. In the *Complete Masters*, the gatefold opens to a poem also titled *A Love Supreme* written by Coltrane along with a letter thanking God and those listening. He was kicked from the Miles Davis quartet for his heroin use and after his spiritual reawakening, he kicked his drug and alcohol habits, as a love letter to spirituality he composed this album. He would carry on experimenting with his composing but the success of the album didn't carry over into Coltrane's follow up records.

Coltrane performing in Copenhagen, Denmark in 1961

Track List

<u>SIDE A</u>
Track 1: Acknowledgement
Track 2: Resolution
<u>SIDE B</u>
Track 1: Pursuance
Track 2: Psalm

Pet Sounds

Beach Boys

Release Date: 1966 | **Record Label:** Capitol

Produced, composed and arranged by Brian Wilson, it is often considered to be a Brian Wilson solo album with the Beach Boys name attached.

In 1965 Wilson withdrew from live performances after suffering form panic attacks, instead he would focus more on composing and recording. After hearing The Beatles' album *Rubber Soul*, Wilson decided to expand on the music he created, coincidentally the music he was inspired to write would then inspire McCartney. *Pet Sounds* is said to have brought on the age of albums, LPs no longer had to be a reason to promote singles, but they could be conceived as a whole piece of work and the singles could promote

the album. Some would say it was *Sgt Pepper* that did this but Beatles' producer George Martin has said that without *Pet Sounds* there would be no *Sgt Pepper*.

The Beach Boys had moved away from the beach theme in the previous album *The Beach Boys Today* and wanted to expand on the sound introduced in that album. The songs in *Pet Sounds* would use instruments not normally associated with the genre such as electro-theremin, bongos and accordions There are psychedelic elements throughout such as the echo, reverb and choice of instruments evoking a dream-like or otherworldly sound, this experimentation with sound and recording has caused debate as to whether *Pet Sounds* should be categorised as

psychedelic rock. The album cost $70,000 to produce, over $500,000 in today's equivalent, which was unheard of in 1966.

On it's release in America the album received a tepid reaction while across the pond in Britain it was praised, remaining in the top ten for six months. A two-disc coloured vinyl set was released in 2006 that includes two mixes of the same album, one stereo mix on a green LP and one mono on translucent yellow.

Track List

SIDE A

Track 1:	Wouldn't It Be Nice
Track 2:	You Still Believe In Me
Track 3:	That's Not Me
Track 4:	Don't Talk (Put Your Head On My Shoulder)
Track 5:	I'm Waiting For The Day
Track 6:	Let's Go Away For Awhile
Track 7:	Sloop John B

SIDE B

Track 1:	God Only Knows
Track 2:	I Know There's An Answer
Track 3:	Here Today
Track 4:	I Just Wasn't Made For These Times
Track 5:	Pet Sounds
Track 6:	Caroline, No

The Beach Boys, 1981

Blonde On Blonde

Bob Dylan

Release Date: 1966 | Record Label: Columbia Records

A very small number of albums change the face of popular music, although critics like to opine that many do so. Wherever you stand, there's no denying that Bob Dylan's seventh studio LP did exactly that. *Blonde On Blonde* was one of the first double albums in popular music; it was Dylan's first to be recorded in Nashville, using the cream of that city's talents as well as his own band; and it completed a trilogy of LPs that he had initiated with *Bringing It All Back Home* (1965) and *Highway 61 Revisited* (1965).

Blonde On Blonde (it seems insulting to abbreviate it to *BOB* — appropriate though that would be) was also the album that consolidated Dylan's recent switch to largely — but not entirely — electric music. It has been widely documented that this move was not universally loved by his fanbase, but let's recap.

Highway 61 Revisited, which contained many electric elements, was released in August 1965; Dylan recorded *Blonde On Blonde* between October the same year and March 1966; in May 1966,

around the time of the new album's release, he played a show at the Free Trade Hall in Manchester where some wag in the crowd shouted "Judas!" in annoyance at his apparently outrageous use of an electric guitar. Thus was the '60s born, goes the received rock wisdom, the birth of the decade in cultural terms being synonymous with musicians breaking free of their assigned categories and doing what the hell they wanted to for the first time.

Cultural significance aside, how does *Blonde On Blonde* stand up after more than 50 years as a body of work? Well, the usual Dylan tropes are all present and correct. His voice may have been raw by the standards of the day, but it was a thing of honeyed beauty compared to the shredded rasp it later became due to the rigours of decades on the road. Then there's Dylan's endless harmonica, which — depending on your point of view — is either an eloquent evocation of roots music and Americana, or a terrible squealing racket that should stop forthwith. Then again, anyone who tends towards the slightly uncharitable latter view probably isn't listening to this

> **"Blonde on Blonde was the album that consolidated Dylan's recent switch to largely electric music"**

Track List

SIDE A
Track 1: Rainy Day Women #12 & 35
Track 2: Pledging My Time
Track 3: Visions Of Johanna
Track 4: One Of Us Must Know (Sooner or Later)

SIDE B
Track 1: I Want You
Track 2: Stuck Inside Of Mobile With The Memphis Blues Again
Track 3: Leopard-Skin Pill-Box Hat
Track 4: Just Like A Woman

SIDE C
Track 1: Most Likely You Go Your Way and I'll Go Mine
Track 2: Temporary Like Achilles
Track 3: Absolutely Sweet Marie
Track 4: 4th Time Around
Track 5: Obviously 5 Believers

SIDE D
Track 1: Sad Eyed Lady Of The Lowlands

music, or even still reading this entry, for that matter.

Right from the off, the album earns its place in the classic '60s canon. Dylan was courageous to kick it off with *'Rainy Day Women #12 & 35'*, a song that not only had a near-unpronounceable title but also rested on the line *"Everybody must get stoned"*. Remember, this was at a point in American judicial history when even mentioning cannabis could earn you a spell in San Quentin and an appointment in the showers with Mr Big. Dylan cleverly avoided such an encounter by cross-referencing the *"stoned"*

part of his lyric with 'stoning' in the Biblical sense, wise man that he was. What's more, setting the song to a Salvation Army-style marching beat and revival-church wails was subversively brilliant.

Then there's *'Visions of Johanna'*, *'I Want You'*, *'Leopard-Skin Pill-Box Hat'*… the list of classic song titles rolls on through the album, these cuts in particular revealing Dylan's expertise at evoking emotions through lyrics. For anyone who has found themselves wondering exactly why it is that Bob Dylan's '60s albums are so revered, the secret is most definitely in these songs; they express with perfect economy the struggles of the human condition. To listen to these songs is to recognise oneself in them.

The album winds to a halt after the 11-minute *'Sad Eyed Lady Of The Lowlands'*, written for Dylan's wife, Sara, and occupying the whole of Side Four. It's an epic ending to a huge body of work, and epitomises the whole album in that it's musically ambitious but thematically uncomplicated — a love song. As a single element of its creator's skills, it's unparalleled, as is *Blonde On Blonde* as a whole. Bob Dylan recorded albums that were more socially critical than this one, and certainly more digestible, but perhaps not as demonstrative of his world view.

OTHER ALBUMS

The Times They Are a-Changin' (1964)
We associate protest music with the late '60s, and forget that before 1965, anti-establishment songs were relatively rare. Back in 1964, Bob was laying down the angry grooves before it became cool — see the title cut of this incendiary album.

Highway 61 Revisited (1965)
Going electric in 1965 with this stunning album, Dylan is said by many to have kickstarted the '60s in doing so. Although not all of his fans appreciated the switch from acoustic music, who can argue with *'Like A Rolling Stone'*?

Blood on the Tracks (1975)
In this astounding, unpredictable suite of songs, the music is emotive and compelling. Just as he had defined the '60s with his first few albums, so Dylan soundtracked the rise of the confessional '70s singer-songwriter with this classic.

Are You Experienced

The Jimi Hendrix Experience

Release Date: 1967 | **Record Label:** Track Records

Often considered one of the greatest albums of all time, and cementing Jimi Hendrix's status as the original guitar hero, *Are You Experienced* remains a significant milestone in the history of rock music over 50 years since its release. Born in Seattle and trying to make a name for himself in New York, Hendrix moved to England under the management of former Animals bassist Chas Chandler in 1966. Within months he had formed a band with bassist Noel Redding and drummer Mitch Mitchell. The newly-christened The Jimi Hendrix Experience had been assembled by Chandler to showcase Hendrix's unique songwriting and guitar wizardry.

Are You Experienced was recorded in 16 sessions over five months at three London Studios — De Lane Lea Studios, CBS and Olympic Studios. Recording for the album was done in between a busy schedule of live performances, though the trio notoriously laid down entire tracks with minimal fuss. Most notably, *'The Wind Cries Mary'* was reportedly recorded in a single take having only been written the night before by Hendrix. Chandler estimated the album cost no more than £1,500 to produce.

The original UK release of the LP in May 1967 featured a mono mix, but a stereo mix was also produced when the record made its way to the US in August of the same year. There are several differences between the two mixes, including a drumroll on *'May This Be Love'* and the sound of Hendrix turning pages of lyrics which are not audible on the mono mix.

As well as wrangling the absolute best from his guitar, Hendrix also introduced the Octavia pedal on the group's debut record — an effects pedal created exclusively for Hendrix by sound technician Roger Mayer to duplicate the guitar sound an octave up or down and add some fuzz. The distinct sound is most iconically used during *'Purple Haze'*. While not solely responsible for the 'wah-wah' sound now common in funk guitar, it was Hendrix's slide technique on *'I Don't Live Today'* which effects pedal manufacturer Vox tried to replicate with the very first 'wah-wah' pedal.

The original UK pressings of *Are You Experienced* are fronted by an image of Hendrix flanked by

> ## "The shot saw the debut of the 'Experience afro', a key part of their signature look"

Track List

SIDE A

Track 1:	Foxy Lady
Track 2:	Manic Depression
Track 3:	Red House
Track 4:	Can You See Me
Track 5:	Love Or Confusion
Track 6:	I Don't Live Today

SIDE D

Track 1:	May This Be Love
Track 2:	Fire
Track 3:	Third Stone From The Sun
Track 4:	Remember
Track 5:	Are You Experienced?

Mitchell and Redding, photographed by Bruce Fleming who had previously worked with The Hollies and The Animals. Inexplicably these initial copies featured no mention of the band's name on the cover, an oversight rectified on further European Polydor-released versions with the addition of 'Jimi Hendrix' above the album title. Hendrix wasn't keen on the record's cover so graphic designer and

fashion photographer Karl Ferris was approached to create a new, more psychedelic cover.

Appearing on the US release three months later, Ferris opted for a yellow cover with pink lettering and an infrared photograph of the band taken through a fisheye lens. The shot was taken at London's Kew Gardens and saw the debut of the 'Experience afro', a key part of the trio's signature look. Ferris described the Experience's music as "so far out that it seemed to have come from outer space," inspiring him to create a backstory for the image of a "group travelling through space in a Biosphere on their way to bring their unworldly space music to earth." Hendrix's jacket in the photo was actually a gift from a fan.

Are You Experienced has featured various distinct track listings since its initial release, most notably originally omitting UK chart hits *'Purple Haze'*, *'Hey Joe'* and *'The Wind Cries Mary'*. The original 11-track listing was altered for the US version, including the three aforementioned UK singles whilst dropping *'Red House'*, *'Can You See Me'* and *'Remember'*. Further releases began to include 17 tracks, although the album's order varies across versions and some tracks' titles differ subtly - such as *'Foxy Lady'/'Foxey Lady'* and *'3rd Stone From The Sun'/'Third Stone From The Sun'*.

OTHER ALBUMS

Axis: Bold as Love (1967)

The Experience's second album, released the same year as their first to fulfill their record contract. Hendrix begins to explore a more mellow sound, such as that on *'Little Wing'*.

Electric Ladyland (1968)

Hendrix's songwriting peaked on this final album with the original Experience. Featuring *'Voodoo Chile'* and *'All Along The Watchtower'*, this boundary-pushing double LP sees the limits of guitar experimentation stretched.

Live at Monterey (2007)

This performance at Monterey Pop Festival in 1967 announced the Experience to America. If Hendrix's supreme stage presence doesn't convince you, otherworldly renditions of *'Wild Thing'* and *'Like A Rolling Stone'* will.

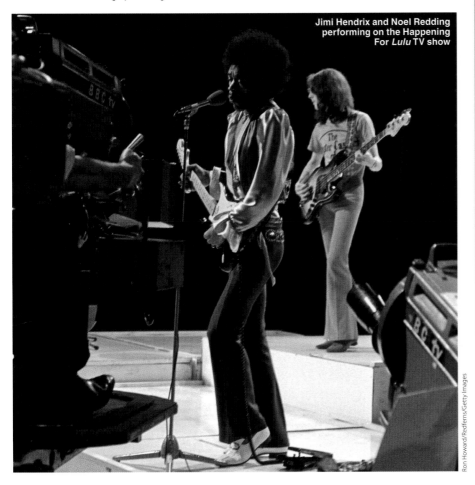

Jimi Hendrix and Noel Redding performing on the Happening For *Lulu* TV show

Ron Howard/Redferns/Getty Images

The Velvet Underground & Nico

The Velvet Underground

Release Date: 1967 | Record Label: Verve

There's typical Warholian humour in the fact that an album as daring, as multifaceted, and as frequently bleak as *The Velvet Underground & Nico* is forever denoted by the garish yellow form of a screen-printed banana. It's testament, also, to the genius of band and artist that both music and art continue to resonate after more than half a century. Even if you haven't heard the former, then you've almost certainly seen the latter.

Maybe it's this disconnect that helps fuel *TVU&N's* somewhat notorious reputation. When The Velvet Underground's debut finally saw the light of day, it was met with a mixture of critical disdain and commercial indifference. Its classic status would gradually be revised and then enshrined over time, but there's a reason this seminal record left all but a small, dedicated audience dumbfounded in 1967.

Or, rather, there are several reasons. Lou Reed's unflinching portrayals of the seediest elements of New York nightlife; John Cale's obsession with creating new soundscapes through his piano and viola; the aural assault of Sterling Morrison and Moe Tucker on guitar and drums respectively. And then there's Nico. Though the German singer was only included at Warhol's behest, she more than justifies her full credit, her deep vocals offering a seductive counterpoint to Reed's almost-spoken chants. Nico's affiliation with the band would end soon after the record's release, but not before she'd made her mark on rock history.

The Velvet Underground would oscillate between dissonance and a more conventional sound on their subsequent records, but it's *TVU&N* that stands as their crowning achievement, its dense, penetrative collage of noise and the two voices of Reed and Nico still able to confound and entrance after all this time. No record collection is complete without it — depending on the pressing, you might even be able to peel your banana — and if nothing else, who doesn't want to have an authentic Warhol to display in their home?

Velvet Underground, 1966

Track List

SIDE A
Track 1: Sunday Morning
Track 2: I'm Waiting For The Man
Track 3: Femme Fatale
Track 4: Venus In Furs
Track 5: Run Run Run
Track 6: All Tomorrow's Parties
SIDE B
Track 1: Heroin
Track 2: There She Goes Again
Track 3: I'll Be Your Mirror
Track 4: The Black Angel's Death Song
Track 5: European Son

At Folsom Prison

Johnny Cash

Release Date: 1968 | **Record Label:** Columbia

Perhaps more than any other popular musician, Johnny Cash felt a kinship with the incarcerated. The Man in Black's life and music were always laced with pain and tragedy, and while he'd spend much of his career playing shows to venues around the world, it was within the more sombre confines of state prisons that his performances often felt most at home.

Though Cash had been performing prison concerts since the late '50s, it wasn't until 1968, and a fortuitous pairing with renowned producer Bob Johnston, that Cash finally got the opportunity to record one for release. A couple of venues were mooted, but one in particular stood out — the inspiration for Cash's signature *'Folsom Prison Blues'*.

At Folsom Prison marked the beginning of a series of live albums performed and recorded behind penitentiary walls — *At San Quentin*, *På Österåker* and *A Concert Behind Prison Walls* would follow — but it remains the most vital. And despite the setting, it's anything but downbeat. The Folsom crowd is raucous but audibly jubilant, and Cash's legendary charisma oozes between songs. He reminds them that the show is being recorded, "so you can't say hell or shit or anything like that," before giving a shout out to Johnston.

Johnny Cash, 1965

Musically, this is Cash at the peak of his powers, his set mixing classic folk and country numbers with a few ballads and even, in *'Send A Picture Of Mother'*, a song written by a Folsom inmate. His voice, as ever, is immaculate, and that distinctive baritone with its delicious Southern drawl captures the longing, rebelliousness, and sometimes resignation of these songs perfectly.

You could stack the shelves of a hefty record collection purely with Cash's oeuvre. But even with almost half a century's worth of recordings to choose from, there's still something particularly thrilling about hearing that customary introduction to *'Folsom Prison Blues'* played for a crowd to which they're all-too familiar.

Track List

SIDE A

Track 1: Folsom Prison Blues
Track 2: Dark As The Dungeon
Track 3: I Still Miss Someone
Track 4: Cocaine Blues
Track 5: 25 Minutes To Go
Track 6: Orange Blossom Special
Track 7: The Long Black Veil

SIDE B

Track 1: Send a Picture Of Mother
Track 2: The Wall
Track 3: Dirty Old Egg-Suckin' Dog
Track 4: Flushed From The Bathroom Of Your Heart
Track 5: Jackson
Track 6: Give My Love To Rose
Track 7: I Got Stripes
Track 8: Green, Green Grass Of Home
Track 9: Greystone Chapel

Sgt. Pepper's Lonely Hearts Club Band

The Beatles

Release Date: 1967 | **Record Label:** Parlophone/Capitol

Before *Sgt. Pepper* **was released in 1967 things were looking bleak for The Beatles.** The band announced in 1966 that they would be retiring from live performances and there were rumours of the band's breakup. All four members taking a three month hiatus didn't help calm the rumours.

When they did get back to the studio and released the single *'Penny Lane'/'Strawberry Fields Forever'* it only reached #2 in the charts, ending The Beatles run of 11 consecutive #1 singles. This led many to think that The Beatles time at the top had ended.

But the fab four would embark on their most ambitious project that would go on to break sales records, despite not having any singles released to promote it. The Beatles, without having to worry about performing the songs live once the album was out, decided to use new recording techniques and technology to expand the sound and create an album no one had ever heard. Paul McCartney became the driving force of the album, he didn't want to make songs that The Beatles would record, instead he wanted to write the music that *Sgt. Pepper* would. As well as evolving their sound the band would alter their appearance to fit the tone of the songs. The black suits and moptops were

Track List

SIDE A

Track 1:	Sgt. Pepper's Lonely Hearts Club Band
Track 2:	With A Little Help From My Friends
Track 3:	Lucy In The Sky With Diamonds
Track 4:	Getting Better
Track 5:	Fixing A Hole
Track 6:	She's Leaving Home
Track 7	Being For The Benefit Of Mr Kite

SIDE B

Track 1:	Within You Without You
Track 2:	When I'm Sixty-Four
Track 3:	Lovely Rita
Track 4:	Good Morning Good Morning
Track 5:	Sgt. Pepper's Lonely Hearts Club Band (Reprise)
Track 6:	A Day In The Life

Gone were the days of black suits and moptops, replaced with bright colours and droopy moustaches

replaced with brightly coloured military uniforms, long hair and drooping moustaches. Because the band was no longer going to be performing live, they recorded *Sgt. Pepper* to sound like it was. Perhaps this is why the first sound you hear in the album is an audience and orchestra tuning and why songs fade into each other, to give the impression that what you are hearing is right there in front of you.

Sgt. Pepper's Lonely Hearts Club Band was the first Beatles album to be released simultaneously around the world and with the same song list. The BBC was quick to ban the song *'A Day In The Life'* due to the lyrics being interpreted as encouraging drug use. The lyric "4,000 holes in Blackburn" was thought to reference holes in the arm of a drug user. While these innuendos were never confirmed or denied by the group, Paul McCartney's response was blunt when he said, "We don't care if they ban our songs. It might help the LP."

Today, *Sgt. Pepper's Lonely Hearts Club Band* is the best selling (non-compilation) album of all time in the UK with over 5 million copies sold and

its album art is one of the most recognisable covers. We wouldn't blame you for thinking that a picture of The Beatles was pasted over a collage of famous people, but in fact life-size cutouts of each individual was made and the band members took a photo among them. They even borrowed the wax figures of themselves from Madame Tussauds. The cover cost at the time £3,000 when the average cost of an album cover at the time was £50.

The Beatles included a couple of things with the vinyl release to make the fan's listening experience at home more interactive. *Sgt. Pepper* was the first rock LP to have the lyrics to their songs printed on the cover, before magazines would usually print them. Original pressings of the Vinyl also came with a piece of card with numerous cut-outs including a dropping moustache, sergeant stripes and a stand of the four Beatles. There are a number of coloured LPs released over the years including a red version, yellow, orange, a Canada-only pink and grey marbled edition as well as a picture disc of the album artwork.

Filming a sequence for *'I Am the Walrus'*

Michael Ochs Archives/Getty Images

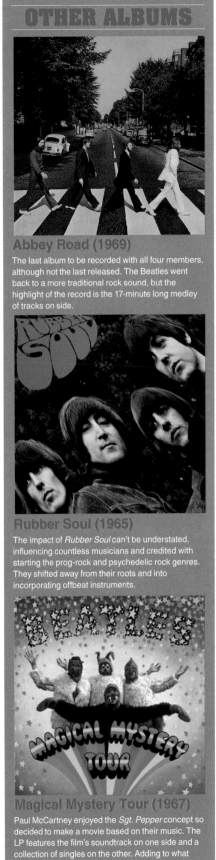

BOB MARLEY & THE WAILERS

Exodus

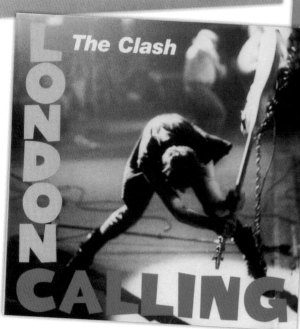
The Clash
LONDON CALLING

NEVER MIND
THE BOLLOC
HERE'S THE
SEX PISTO

SIMON
AND
GARFUNKEL
Bridge
Over
Troubled
Water

LOU REED-TRANSFORMER

FLEETWOOD MAC
RUMOURS

GOODBYE YELLOW BRICK ROAD
ELTON JOHN

Bill Wit
AT CARNE

'70S

Led Zeppelin III

Led Zeppelin

Release Date: 1970 | Record Label: Atlantic

Led Zeppelin weren't quite the biggest band in the world by the time they released their third album, but they were well on their way. Thanks to extended concert tours in America, they had a huge fanbase who loved the massive riffs of guitarist Jimmy Page and the unearthly vocal squeals of Robert Plant. The rhythm section of bassist John Paul Jones and drummer John Bonham were no slouches, of course, but Zep were all about Page and Plant in the wider public's eyes — and in reality Zep were guided by Page and no-one else.

This explains the direction which *Led Zeppelin III* took. While Zep's debut album and the follow-up, both released in 1969, had essentially been LPs of hard rock songs with a few acoustic parts here and there, *III* was mostly unplugged. A calmer, sweeter, more relaxed vibe permeated the record as a result, itself aided by the fact that Page and Plant composed the songs in a remote Welsh cottage called Bron-Yr-Aur. With no running water or electricity, the twosome pulled out acoustic guitars, began writing — and in doing so established the great rock tradition of 'getting it together in the country'.

Sit back in your beanbag, slap some headphones on and immerse yourself in the opening cut, *'Immigrant Song'* — the heaviest song on the album. Page's classic octave-based guitar riff chimes in, while Plant delivers the wail for which he had already become famous. Singing of the *"land of ice and snow"*, his outlandish sentiments and shrieks seem plausible in this setting. Friends is a deeper song, despite being largely acoustic: where it excels is with its unusual orchestration of Indian-sounding strings.

'Celebration Day' is rock 'n' roll, but a strange variant of that genre: Plant's vocals are initially low and intoned — a welcome change from his standard shredded-throat performance — and Page seems to be entering cowboy country territory at times. It's an interesting diversion, though, followed by a breathtaking left turn into stripped-down blues territory.

'Since I've Been Loving You' is basically a slow blues jam lasting seven minutes, focusing

> **"In doing so established the great rock tradition of 'getting it together in the country'"**

Track List

SIDE A

Track 1:	Immigrant Song
Track 2:	Friends
Track 3:	Celebration Day
Track 4:	Since I've Been Loving You
Track 5:	Out On The Tiles

SIDE B

Track 1:	Gallows Pole
Track 2:	Tangerine
Track 3:	That's The Way
Track 4:	Bron-Y-Aur Stomp
Track 5:	Hats Off To (Roy) Harper

The lack of electricity where they wrote most of the album lent itself to the more acoustic sounds

almost entirely on a workout for Plant's belt-vocal technique and practically unaccompanied soloing from Page. Sure, you might dismiss the song as a mere technique-fest, but you'd be missing the very real feel that the two master musicians injected into the performance. Led Zeppelin were nothing if not emotional in their music, after all — hence the connection they enjoyed with their audiences.

If you were to write a parody of a Led Zep song that mirrored their trademark stop-start riffing, you might well come up with *'Out On The Tiles'*. Blustering, breathless and not radically better than or different to any of the other heavy songs in Zep's catalogue, it ends the riff-focused first side of *III* with a bang. Flip the vinyl and the acoustic fun really begins.

'Gallows Pole' is just beautiful. When Page picked up an acoustic guitar, which he did in six- and 12-string variants on this LP for maximum

expression, he gave the heavy rock world the gift of subtlety. There's not a power ballad on here — they weren't invented for another few years — but there are certainly songs which build from wispy acoustic chords to a bigger sound by their end. *'Gallows Pole'* is the first of these, followed by *'Tangerine'*, which ends with a sweet country vibe. *'That's The Way'* and *'Bron-Y-Aur Stomp'* reinforce the message too, and the LP ends with *'Hats Off To (Roy) Harper'*, a slightly anticlimactic bit of experimenting. Plant's vocals are unusually treated in the studio, and Page's slide guitar dominates, but the real gold is to be had earlier on in the record.

We all agree that *III* is a splendid album nowadays, but critics just didn't get it at the time. Neither heavy enough for headbangers nor progressive enough for Jethro Tull fans, it fell between two stools, it was thought. How wrong they were, and how wonderful hindsight is.

Barack Obama talks with the surviving members of Led Zeppelin John Paul Jones, Robert Plant and Jimmy Page during intermission at the Kennedy Center Honors

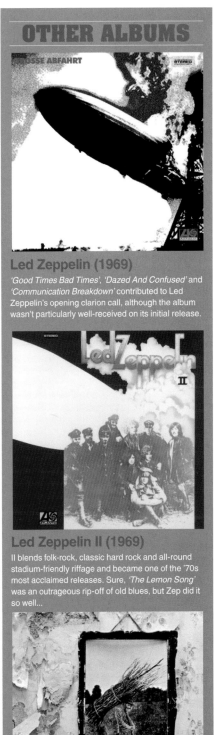

OTHER ALBUMS

Led Zeppelin (1969)

'Good Times Bad Times', *'Dazed And Confused'* and *'Communication Breakdown'* contributed to Led Zeppelin's opening clarion call, although the album wasn't particularly well-received on its initial release.

Led Zeppelin II (1969)

II blends folk-rock, classic hard rock and all-round stadium-friendly riffage and became one of the '70s most acclaimed releases. Sure, *'The Lemon Song'* was an outrageous rip-off of old blues, but Zep did it so well...

Led Zeppelin IV (1971)

"And she's buying a stairway to hea-vunnnn..." Yes, you couldn't escape Led Zep in 1971 thanks to their best-known song, a sprawling epic that was just one amazing track on this album. The classic songs just kept coming.

Pete Souza/The White House/Getty Images

Paranoid

Black Sabbath

Release Date: 1970 | **Record Label:** Vertigo

As anyone who likes unsociably loud music will tell you, heavy metal is popularly thought to have been born in 1970 when Brummie headbangers Black Sabbath released their self-titled debut album. Let's go one further and suggest that heavy metal really hit its stride for the first time with Sabbath's second album, *Paranoid*, a heavier, more threatening and more nuanced collection of songs.

Committed metal fans of a certain age — shall we say, between 40 and 60 as you read this — know the eight-song tracklisting off by heart. The one-two opening shot of *'War Pigs'* and *'Paranoid'* itself simply cannot be bettered in the metal world. The former, a critique of warfare and in particular of the American government's policies regarding Vietnam, sees lyricist and bassist Geezer Butler on peak form — even if he can't find a better way to rhyme 'masses' than with itself in the couplet *"Generals gathered in their masses/Just like witches at black masses"*. The latter, a zippy paean to mental instability, is probably Sabbath's best-known song, executed at a rare, non-doomy tempo. The album then moves on to the sensuous instrumental *'Planet Caravan'*, a beautiful, landscaped song, before the pulverising hammer blow of *'Iron Man'*.

Sabbath's psychedelic and blues influences reveal themselves in *'Electric Funeral'* and *'Hand Of Doom'*, the latter simultaneously terrifying and enthralling listeners with its sinister, bass-only introduction. The album winds up with *'Rat Salad'* — an energetic instrumental — and *'Fairies Wear Boots'*, said to be inspired by threats from a skinhead gang. It's not sheer power that makes *Paranoid* a unique album, although it has that to spare: it's the keen awareness of songwriting dynamics displayed by Butler plus singer Ozzy Osbourne, guitarist Tony Iommi and Bill Ward, all still in their very early 20s at the time of recording. That a record such as this was written and delivered by such young musicians is nothing short of miraculous, albeit in the infernal rather than heavenly sense.

Track List

SIDE A
Track 1: War Pigs
Track 2: Paranoid
Track 3: Planet Caravan
Track 4: Iron Man
SIDE B
Track 1: Electric Funeral
Track 2: Hand Of Doom
Track 3: Rat Salad
Track 4: Fairies Wear Boots

Toni Iommi in 1978

Black Sabbath, 1970

Bridge Over Troubled Water

Simon & Garfunkel

Release Date: 1970 | **Record Label:** Columbia

Paul Simon and Art Garfunkel were a folk duo in the same way that The Beatles were a rock band. The couple could do folk, for sure, but there was so much more to their talents than a simple genre tag.

Masters of close vocal arrangement and harmony, the twosome covered huge amounts of musical ground, always bewitchingly accomplished and rarely equalled. Also like The Beatles, Simon & Garfunkel's career together was cut short by personality clashes that were the result of a surfeit of talent.

Bridge Over Troubled Water was the duo's fifth and final album, but is in no way a negative or conflicted collection of songs. This could well be, of course,

because Simon wrote all the songs; Garfunkel contributed his usual expert vocals, but his attention was reportedly on his then-burgeoning film career. If this is the case, his lack of focus was to everyone else's gain, because the album contains the duo's two best-known songs — the title track and *'The Boxer'*, as well as the still-astounding *'La Condor Pasa (If I Could)'*, which foretold Simon's immense success a decade later with the Afrobeat-influenced *'Graceland'*.

The song *'Bridge Over Troubled Water'* has been besmirched a little in recent years thanks to far too many earnest charity renditions, and worse, reality-TV singing contests'. Still, forget all that: the still-unsurpassed original is a thing of orchestrated, dynamic beauty, from its simple opening statement to the huge, Phil Spector-esque wall of sound which finishes it.

Then there's *'The Boxer'*, a splendid showcase for Simon & Garfunkel's greatest asset — their close harmonies, sung in a meaningless but compelling *"Lie-la-lie... lie-la-lie-lie, lie-la-lie"* that sounds perfect at high volume. Another standout cut is *'Cecilia'*, the most energetic love song ever recorded, and, like *'La Condor Pasa'*, recorded with an unorthodox, Latin-flavoured feel. The album sounds fresh and innovative, even to this day: if you listen to any modern acoustic folk artist, you'll hear its ongoing influence.

'Cecilia' and *'Bridge Over Trouble Water'* feel like two of the most-covered songs ever

Track List

SIDE A
Track 1: Bridge Over Troubled Water
Track 2: La Condor Pasa (If I Could)
Track 3: Cecilia
Track 4: Keep The Customer Satisfied
Track 5: So Long, Frank Lloyd Wright

SIDE B
Track 1: The Boxer
Track 2: Baby Driver
Track 3: The Only Living Boy In New York
Track 4: Why Don't You Write Me
Track 5: Bye Bye Love
Track 6: Song For The Asking

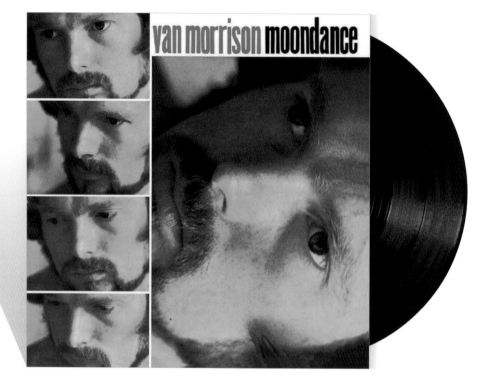

Moondance

Van Morrison

Release Date: 1970 | Record Label: Warner Bros.

It seemed, for a brief time following the release of Astral Weeks, that Van Morrison might eschew mainstream success altogether. *'Brown Eyed Girl'* was, and still is, a phenomenal hit, but the singer-songwriter's follow-up LP was an esoteric fusion of jazz, blues and soul that neither the public nor Warner Bros. immediately took to. Then came *Moondance*.

Morrison's third album made his previous work seem like a calibration test, taking the immediacy and unshakeable catchiness of his early singles and combining it with the experimentalism and sophistication of *Astral Weeks*. *Moondance* is once again a blend of musical styles, but above all it's a sublime pop album, crammed with hooks and melodies that Morrison and his band reel off with panache and an enviable ease.

Opener *'And It Stoned Me'* recounts a transformative experience where a young Morrison was overwhelmed by a bucolic scene in his native Northern Ireland, the soulful vocals expressing a reverence for nature that recurs throughout the record. On the title track, Morrison's blues stylings are infused with the jazzy sounds of flute, piano and saxophone, but once again he sounds effortless among them. As he demonstrates throughout

Moondance, Van's inimitable vocal style transitions easily between rugged and lyrical, hard and velvet-smooth, often within the space of a single song, as on *'Brand New Day'*.

And while the harmonious tapestry of vocals, guitar and brass give *Moondance* its most stellar

Morrison performs in 1976 at The Band's final concert

Track List

SIDE A
Track 1:	And It Stoned Me
Track 2:	Moondance
Track 3:	Crazy Love
Track 4:	Caravan
Track 5:	Into The Mystic

SIDE B
Track 1:	Come Running
Track 2:	These Dreams Of You
Track 3:	Brand New Day
Track 4:	Everyone
Track 5:	Glad Tidings

moments, Morrison's lyrics are no less integral. Veering between the vivid and the abstract, they reflect influences spanning everything from Irish folk songs to romantic poetry. Nowhere is this lyrical mastery better showcased than at the close of Side A. On the gorgeous *'Into The Mystic'*, Morrison's more spiritual and folk-inflected songwriting comes to the fore: *"Hark, now hear the sailors cry/Smell the sea and feel the sky/Let your soul and spirit fly/Into the mystic."* Few records capture that fleeting feeling between earthly sensation and spiritual transcendence. *Moondance* is one of them.

Blue

Joni Mitchell

Release Date: 1971 | **Record Label:** Reprise

Mitchell performing at the Universal Amphitheatre in 1974

photograph August 1974

Such is its brilliance that calling *Blue*, Joni Mitchell's fourth LP and her first true masterpiece, "the greatest break-up album of all time" would still be selling it short. It's a heartrending collection of songs about love and loss, sure, but it's also so much more than that.

Taking inspiration from several love affairs, but particularly the end of her relationship with Graham Nash, the record arrived at a time when both fame and more personal matters were proving too much for the Canadian singer-songwriter to take. Following her separation from Nash, Mitchell escaped the touring bubble of North America to spend time in, among other remote locales, some inhabited caves above Matala in Crete. These modest surroundings provided the backdrop for a series of remarkably candid folk songs, each an unfiltered window into the heart of their author.

But despite all this baggage, *Blue* is anything but overwrought. It's pared down, intimate — its ten songs lasting a little over 35 minutes. Stripped of any embellishment or intrusive production, all that you're left with are a few fleeting piano melodies, the strumming of a guitar or dulcimer, and Mitchell's utterly bewitching vocals. The arrangements on the record are delicate, and deceptively intricate, but the

Track List

SIDE A
Track 1: All I Want
Track 2: My Old Man
Track 3: Little Greeny
Track 4: Carey
Track 5: Blue
SIDE B
Track 1: California
Track 2: This Flight Tonight
Track 3: River
Track 4: A Case Of You
Track 5: The Last Time I Saw Richard

emotions are painfully raw.

Mitchell's later records would often lean towards the experimental and unconventional, but *Blue* remains the purest example of her genius. It's positively overflowing with heartache, hurt and angst, but Mitchell's unparalleled ability to take these feelings and distil them into perfectly formed tunes sets it apart. And while there are many artists and albums whose soul-searching, melancholy sounds are worthy of your collection, none of them can match *Blue* for its articulations on the intoxicating, bittersweet nature of love.

What's Going On

Marvin Gaye

Release Date: 1971 | Record Label: Tamla

Marvin Gaye's 1971 landmark album represented a dramatic change in lyrical content and musical style, an awakening which would revolutionise black music. *What's Going On* was the eleventh record released by the soul legend, regularly appearing in Greatest Album lists owing to its astute social commentary and cultural significance. The self-produced masterpiece brought Gaye's closely held beliefs to the fore, exploring several key issues plaguing society at the time — poverty, racial discrimination, drug abuse, the environment, political corruption and the conflict in Vietnam. The latter particularly close to Gaye's heart, emotionally scarred by letters he'd been receiving from his brother experiencing the warfare first-hand. In fact the entire album is framed through the eyes of a Vietnam war veteran returning to the US, only to find a country divided by hatred. *What's Going On*, is entirely intended as statement.

Released on Tamla Records, *What's Going On* was initially met with resistance from Motown boss Berry Gordy. After the album's title track was released at the beginning of 1971 without Gordy's knowledge, *'What's Going On'* became the fastest selling single for the label and ultimately lead to the full record's release. In a continued break from the norm, Gaye's seminal LP was the first of Motown's releases to fully and individually credit the Funk Brothers — the label's house band.

The album's immediate critical and commercial success guaranteed future creative control over his work and opened the door for his label-mates to do the same, most notably Stevie Wonder.

Presented as a gatefold to show off the family photo montage printed inside, *What's Going On* sleeve shares a remarkably similar layout to that of The Beatles' *Sgt. Pepper*. Early copies of the LP were pressed on Dynaflex vinyl, a short-lived format intended to be thinner and more durable than regular platters that was discontinued later in the '70s.

Marvin Gaye c.1982

Track List

SIDE A
Track 1: What's Going On
Track 2: What's Happening Brother
Track 3: Flyin' High (In The Friendly Sky)
Track 4: Save The Children
Track 5: God Is Love
Track 6: Mercy Mercy Me (The Ecology)

SIDE B
Track 1: Right On
Track 2: Wholy Holy
Track 3: Inner City Blues
(Make Me Wanna Holler)

Sticky Fingers

The Rolling Stones

Release Date: 1971 | **Record Label:** Rolling Stones Records

No record collector wants sticky fingers on vinyl. *Sticky Fingers* on vinyl, however, is a different story. Recorded over two years in three locations (Muscle Shoals Sound Studio in Alabama, frontman Mick Jagger's own country home and Olympic Studios in London), *Sticky Fingers* was the first LP by The Rolling Stones to be released on their own Rolling Stones Records. The album is also the first to feature Mick Taylor, who replaced guitarist Brian Jones in 1969. Amongst the handful of guest musicians to appear on the record, The Who's Pete Townsend is perhaps the most notable, believed to have contributed backing vocals to Sway. The band's ninth record experienced tremendous success, achieving triple platinum certification in the US and topping the charts both sides of the Atlantic.

As well as being revered as one of The Rolling Stones' best, *Sticky Fingers* boasts one of the most classic album covers in rock. The artwork — concepted by renowned artist Andy Warhol — was photographed by Billy Name and features a fully-working zip on most original pressings. Due to the LP's unique construction, hidden underneath the cover art is a second print of presumably the same model stripped down underpants embellished with Warhol's name and the curious line: "This photograph may not be — etc." The model was believed to be Jagger upon the record's release, though is now known not to be the case. The identity of the crotch's owner remains a mystery. And though only small on the reverse of the record, *Sticky Fingers* was the first time The Rolling Stones' now iconic tongue and lips logo had been used. Atlantic Records, who were responsible for the album's Spanish release, insisted the cover art be replaced with a less 'offensive' alternative. It duly was — the LP instead being fronted by a woman's hand emerging from a tin of treacle. In 2015, *Sticky Fingers* received a remastered, fully-unzippable deluxe reissue on 180g heavyweight wax featuring alternative recordings and live tracks.

Track List

SIDE A
Track 1: Brown Sugar
Track 2: Sway
Track 3: Wild Horses
Track 4: Can't You Hear Me Knocking
Track 5: You Gotta Move
SIDE B
Track 1: I Got The Blues
Track 2: Sister Morphine
Track 3: Dead Flowers
Track 4: Moonlight Mile

The Rolling Stones at Summerfest in Milwaukee 2015

The Rise And Fall Of Ziggy Stardust And The Spiders From Mars

David Bowie

Release Date: 1972 | Record Label: RCA Recordsl

Bowie was always open to switching genres album to album, from his early baroque pop in his debut record to Zeppelin-inspired rock in *The Man Who Sold The World.* This free approach to genre allowed him, to capitalise on what was hot, but Bowie would always take a genre and make it his own. With *The Rise And Fall Of Ziggy Stardust And The Spiders From Mars*, Bowie wasn't following a trend, he was establishing himself as the figurehead of a new one: Glam rock. Taking inspiration from Japanese Kabuki theatre and New York fringe music, Bowie would reinvent himself again as the iconic character Ziggy Stardust, a rock star who becomes a messenger for alien beings. The idea of the Ziggy Stardust character was conceived while Bowie was in New York touring for his previous album, *Hunky Dory*. According to Bowie in a 1990 radio interview he had recorded a number of tracks from the Ziggy

album before *Hunky Dory* was even released in 1971.

The album, often shortened to *Ziggy Stardust*, tells the story of the titular Ziggy, who is used by extraterrestrial creatures to spread the word of love and hope before the world is wiped out. The album starts with the song *'Five Years'* in which Ziggy warns humanity of the planet's impeding death. Not all is doom and gloom as the track *'Starman'* tells of a messenger who bring hope to the people of Earth.

The songs don't play as your typical rock album, they sound like they could have been the soundtrack to a musical stage show rather than a rock concert. Bowie, a man who could sing in different ways due to switching music styles in each album he had recorded, changed his vocal style again for Ziggy, most notably in *'Soul Love'*, making it sound like it isn't Bowie singing.

A fan of acting, Bowie dyed his hair bright reddish-brown and dressed in abstract costume. When he

> ## "You weren't seeing a David Bowie concert, it was a Ziggy Stardust performance"

Track List

SIDE A
Track 1: Five Years
Track 2: Soul Love
Track 3: Moonage Daydream
Track 4: Starman
Track 5: It Ain't Easy
SIDE B
Track 1: Lady Stardust
Track 2: Star
Track 3: Hang On To Yourself
Track 4: Ziggy Stardust
Track 5: Suffragette City
Track 6: Rock 'N' Roll Suicide

would perform as Ziggy Stardust, he became the character. When you saw the show you weren't seeing a David Bowie concert, it was a Ziggy Stardust performance. The album, in a similar vein, isn't David Bowie record, it's a Ziggy Stardust record, he just happens to be played by Bowie. His backing band, which he had recorded his previous albums with, were given the name 'the Spiders From Mars'.

The music starts with an acoustic rock sound before moving onto Glam rock when the album reaches *'Hang On To Yourself'*. Then there is a hint of classic '60s rock sprinkled in throughout, such as in *'It Ain't Easy'*, before going back to the acoustic ballad sound the album started with. On the back of the vinyl's cover in the bottom-left corner it says, "To be played at maximum volume", which was omitted from later releases.

David Bowie played concerts as Ziggy for 18 months, touring Britain and the States before deciding to put an end the character. He would release a follow-up album, *Aladdin Sane*, before Ziggy announced unexpectedly at a show in Hammersmith in 1973 that the gig would be their last performance ever before playing *'Rock 'N' Roll Suicide'*. Footage from the Hammersmith show was used in a documentary and concert film also titled *Ziggy Stardust And The Spiders From Mars*. Bowie would then break away from the Spiders from Mars. Despite being a small part of his career, it is still the most iconic.

Bowie would perform as Ziggy Stardust for over a year until retiring the character

OTHER ALBUMS

Hunky Dory (1971)

The success of *Ziggy Stardust* brought fans attention to what Bowie considered his most important album. Bowie experimented with folk, rock and even a bit of Glam before he would go full-out the following year with *Ziggy Stardust*.

Aladdin Sane (1973)

Expanding on the story of Glam icon, the album was dubbed by Bowie as "Ziggy Goes to America", as the songs focus on his experiences as he toured the country. The US influence is also shown in the song's emphasis on rock and blues.

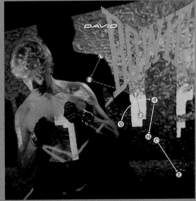

Let's Dance (1983)

Bowie would reinvent himself again, this time working with Chic's Nile Rodgers on a dance-pop album. Mixing funk and dance Bowie would reach mega stardom again with *Let's Dance*, a regular in discos for years after its release.

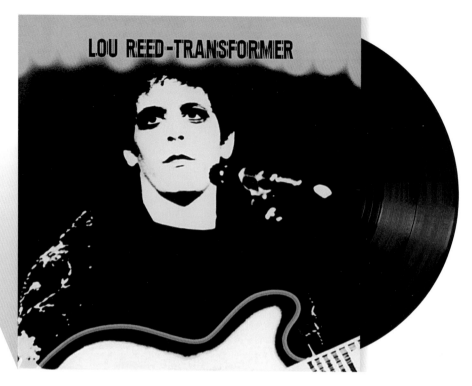

Transformer

Lou Reed

Release Date: 1972 | Record Label: RCA

Most of the life of the unique Lou Reed was so far removed from most ordinary people's experience that it begs belief. The path which the late songwriter followed towards his second solo album, *Transformer*, included a troubled youth in which he was given electroshock therapy to 'treat' his homosexuality; a classic Lower East Side, New York period in which he formed the Velvet Underground and became close to Andy Warhol; and friendships with David Bowie and his guitarist in the Spiders From Mars, Mick Ronson. Add all this up and you're presented with the guy on the cover of the album — a glam-rock icon who positively glowed with deviant beauty. *Transformer's* themes are sexual, forceful and challenging. The big hit was *'Walk On The Wild Side'*, with its five verses each dedicated to a member of Warhol's coterie. With its acoustic whimsy, soulful backing vocals and an immediately identifiable sliding bass motif by English session musician Herbie Flowers, the song was nothing like Reed's usual songwriting style — but it announced his presence to the world in no uncertain terms.

Then there's *'Perfect Day'*, a love song to the most pernicious drug in the world, heroin. With its ethereal tales of visiting the zoo and transcending the self, the song made taking smack sound like a wonderful thing to do. Little wonder the establishment recoiled — at least until 25 years later, when the BBC recorded a huge-selling charity version. The song was so deeply rehabilitated (pun intended) that Reed regularly performed it live in

Lou Reed was a glam rock icon

concert, dropping *'Walk On The Wild Side'* in its place.

Three years and four more albums later, Reed had largely dropped his gender-challenging approach and moved into experimental electronica and rock music, rather like his mentor Bowie, who did exactly the same thing. Commercial success greeted both men in abundance, but for both sets of fans, there remained an understandable nostalgia for the old days. Any discussion of sexual politics in modern rock music owes Reed a favour.

Track List

SIDE A
Track 1: Vicious
Track 2: Andy's Chest
Track 3: Perfect Day
Track 4: Hangin' 'Round
Track 5: Walk On The Wild Side
SIDE B
Track 1: Make Up
Track 2: Satellite Of Love
Track 3: Wagon Wheel
Track 4: New York Telephone Conversation
Track 5: I'm So Free
Track 6: Goodnight Ladies

Harvest

Neil Young

Release Date: 1972 | **Record Label:** Reprise

In 1972 Neil Young, then 26, was already a star in American country, folk and rock circles, thanks to a major hit with his 1970 album *After The Gold Rush*, plus earlier recordings with Crosy, Stills & Nash, Buffalo Springfield and Crazy Horse.

However, when he released *Harvest* in '72, he was elevated to the status of household name, largely because of the hugely-acclaimed songs *'Heart Of Gold'* and *'The Needle And The Damage Done'*. The former is more easily digestible and catchier; the latter is darker, more gloomy in tone and production because it was recorded live, and also better. As is so often the case, *Harvest* was not supposed to launch Young into the stratosphere. It later emerged that

he had recorded the songs spontaneously, on being invited to visit Quadrafonic Studios in Nashville. The songs had been written already, but Young had no band and no rehearsal time: he simply picked whoever was available that night, it being a weekend when most musicians are busy.

The results spoke for themselves. *'Are You Ready For The Country?'* became a signature song for Young, while *'Old Man'* — written for the caretaker at Young's ranch — was a simple, inspiring acoustic singalong that has enticed many a Neil Young novice into his catalogue. *'The Needle And The Damage Done'*, recorded in concert at UCLA the previous year, was a paean to those of Young's friends who had succumbed to heroin overdoses, in particular his previous bassist Danny Whitten. It ends suddenly, halfway through a chord sequence, lending this otherwise slick album a threatening edge.

Critics didn't give *Harvest* particularly good reviews at the time of its release: some felt that he was repeating the *After The Gold Rush* formula a little too readily. However, in years to come the album was recognised as an all-time classic — even by the members of Lynyrd Skynyrd, whose song *'Sweet Home Alabama'* was written in response to some anti-Southern sentiments expressed by Young in the song *'Alabama'*.

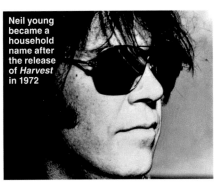

Neil young became a household name after the release of *Harvest* in 1972

Track List

SIDE A
Track 1: Out On The Weekend
Track 2: Harvest
Track 3: A Man Needs A Maid
Track 4: Heart Of Gold
Track 5: Are You Ready For The Country?

SIDE B
Track 1: Old Man
Track 2: There's A World
Track 3: Alabama
Track 4: The Needle And The Damage Done
Track 5: Words (Between The Lines Of Age)

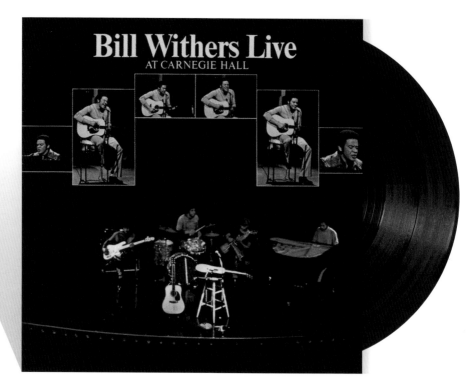

Live At Carnegie Hall

Bill Withers

Release Date: 1973 | **Record Label:** Sussex

You are able to sense the Carnegie Hall audience's love for soul singer Bill Withers when, at a gig on 6 October 1972, he prefaces his song *'Grandma's Hands'* with a long and funny story about his late grandmother; at the end of each line, they applaud with genuine laughter.

This was one of those very rare live gigs — an occasion when all of the performers and

Withers performed throughout the '70s and '80s

spectators are one, thanks to the warm, emotional music on the bill. Fortunately for us, they captured it all on tape.

The big hits are *'Ain't No Sunshine'* and *'Lean On Me'*, and both sound fantastic in this setting. Withers emotes throughout, lending the immortal lines great vigour without going over the top; indeed, the songs' most notable feature is their stripped-down nature. Withers' band was formed of the cream of the early-'70s' soul scene, specifically from the Watts 103rd Street Rhythm Band. These guys, young and hungry though they were back in 1972, knew exactly when to play up and when to lay back again, like all the best musicians. Check out the song *'For My Friend'*, based on a slick guitar, organ and bass riff atop a simple drum beat; the band allows Withers to improvise over its groove with enormous precision and clarity.

Withers himself was only in his early '30s at the time of the recording of *Live At Carnegie Hall*; his performance of the set, and his connection with his audience, were assured and developed. However, he sounds young, fresh and energetic, as do the songs he performs, some of which may have become dulled through endless repetition in subsequent decades. That is the genius of this

album: it brings the listener classic songs that still have their sparkle, delivered by musicians at the peak of their powers. Withers went on to enjoy a long and productive career after this album, although it remained his only in-concert release — perhaps he knew that it couldn't be bettered.

Track List

SIDE A
Track 1: Use Me
Track 2: Friend Of Mine
Track 3: Ain't No Sunshine
Track 4: Grandma's Hands
SIDE B
Track 1: World Keeps Going Around
Track 2: Let Me In Your Life
Track 3: Better Off Dead
Track 4: For My Friend
SIDE C
Track 1: I Can't Write Left Handed
Track 2: Lean On Me
Track 3: Lonely Town Lonely Street
Track 4: Hope She'll Be Happier
SIDE D
Track 1: Let Us Love
Track 2: Harlem/Cold Baloney

Goodbye Yellow Brick Road

Elton John

Release Date: 1973 | Record Label: DJM

Even the most devoted fan would probably admit that Sir Elton John has spent the last 40 years failing to match up to the albums he released between **1970 and 1975.** Specifically, his 1973 album *Goodbye Yellow Brick Road (GYBR)* and 1975's *Captain Fantastic and the Brown Dirt Cowboy* were landmark releases from this period of ambitious creativity, which he has never equalled. We can forgive him this, of course, partly because he is a national treasure but mostly because the music is so great. On *GYBR*, the better known of the two masterpieces, he deployed his splendid piano skills and vocals — yet to sink into the baritone range they occupied on later hits such as, say, *'Nikita'* — in perfect synch with lyricist Bernie Taupin's immortal words.

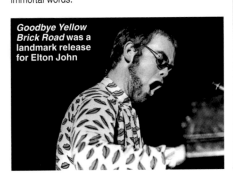

Goodbye Yellow Brick Road was a landmark release for Elton John

Let's get past the big hit *'Candle In The Wind'*, now the biggest-selling song in the known universe since Elton sang a modified version of it at Princess Diana's funeral in 1997. It's a song for the ages all right, even in its original form as a eulogy to the late Marilyn Monroe, but surpassed on the album by its title track and the terrific *'Saturday Night's Alright For Fighting'*. Adopted by heavy-metal bands such as WASP, perhaps because of its aggressive title and speedy tempo, the latter song epitomises a certain night-out-on-the-tiles vibe that Duran Duran matched a decade later, and Oasis a few years later still.

GYBR is a double album, so Elton fans will have their own favourites among the deeper cuts, but we'd definitely point to the very first song, *'Funeral For A Friend/Love Lies Bleeding'*, as one to conjure with. Then there's *'Bennie and the Jets'* (alternately spelled *'Benny & The Jets'* on the label), *'Social Disease'*, *'Grey Seal'*… Elton was unstoppable back then, riding a wave of creativity matched only by his contemporary Stevie Wonder.

Track List

SIDE A
Track 1: Funeral For A Friend/Love Lies Bleeding
Track 2: Candle In The Wind
Track 3: Bennie And The Jets

SIDE B
Track 1: Goodbye Yellow Brick Road
Track 2: This Song Has No Title
Track 3: Grey Seal
Track 4: Jamaica Jerk-Off
Track 5: I've Seen That Movie Toot

SIDE C
Track 1: Sweet Painted Lady
Track 2: The Ballad Of Danny Bailey (1909-34)
Track 3: Dirty Little Girl
Track 4: All The Girls Love Alice

SIDE D
Track 1: Your Sister Can't Twist (But She Can Rock 'N' Roll)
Track 2: Saturday Night's Alright For Fightin
Track 3: Roy Rogers
Track 4: Social Disease
Track 5: Harmony

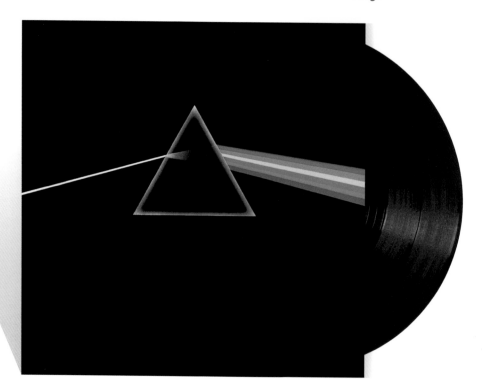

The Dark Side Of The Moon

Pink Floyd

Release Date: 1973 | **Record Label:** Abbey Road Studios/Harvest

Even if you've never listened to *The Dark Side Of The Moon* you'll instantly recognise its incredibly distinctive cover art. The striking piece by Hipgnosis and George Hardie has adorned countless pieces of merchandise over the years and has been a source of inspiration for numerous parodies, ranging from The Simpsons' achingly clever 'Dark Side Of The Moon Pie' to Richard Cheese's hilarious 'The Sunny Side Of The Moon', which swaps out the iconic glass prism for a martini glass.

The prism of light continues through the album's gatefold, which also features a visual representation of the heartbeat that was used by the band throughout the album's runtime. The distinctive design was one of seven that Hipgnosis created and represents the band's legendary use of stage lights, Richard Wright's request for a 'simple and bold' design, as well as the album's lyrics (which for the first time, were actually printed in the album). It's an exceptional piece of art and one of the most recognisable album covers in

> **"You'll hear them discussing how it synchs to The Wizard Of Oz if you play it backwards..."**

modern rock and you're just as likely to see it framed on some hipster's wall as you are to find it in their record collection. You'll probably hear them discussing how it (allegedly) synchs to *The Wizard Of Oz* if you play it backwards as well...

Pink Floyd had always been experimental in its approach to music, but the group really wanted to push the envelope further with its new project and suitably enhance the psychedelic-driven sounds that had featured so heavily on its earlier albums. The group toured *The Dark Side Of The Moon* in two parts, one before the release of the final album, and then a second leg, which took place after the album was released. It seems an incredibly bold move and it's hard to imagine a big artist doing it today, but then Pink Floyd wasn't your typical band and it continued to push away from the group it had been under the guidance of ex founding member, Syd Barrett. Although he officially left Pink Floyd on 6 April 1968, the impact of Barrett can still be felt on *The Dark Side Of The Moon*, most notably in its themes surrounding mental illness (it's thought that Barrett suffered from schizophrenia).

Track List

SIDE A
Track 1:	Speak To Me
Track 2:	Breathe In The Air
Track 3:	On The Run
Track 4:	Time
Track 5:	The Great Gig In The Sky

SIDE B
Track 1:	Money
Track 2:	Us And Them
Track 3:	Any Colour You Like
Track 4:	Brain Damage
Track 5:	Eclipse

Pink Floyd performing at Live 8 London in 2005

MJ Kim/Getty Images

Pink Floyd's album wasn't just content to tackle mental illness though, it also tackles the topics of greed, the passage of time and conflict, all of which feature heavily in songs such as *'Money'*, *'Us And Them'* and *'Brain Damage'* (which was originally known as *'Lunatic'* during the album's recording sessions and live performances). It's arguably one of the most accessible pieces of work that the band has made and has become the perfect starting point for anyone new to the group. It has influenced a huge number of bands as diverse as Radiohead, My Morning Jacket and The Flaming Lips, who re-imagined the album in 2009.

It was a gigantic success for Pink Floyd in the United States where it stayed in the charts for a phenomenal 741 weeks (interestingly, it only spent a single week at #1). Amazingly, it never even reached #1 in the UK (it was held off the top spot by *20 Flash Back Greats From The Sixties*) but that small omission never stopped it from becoming the UK's seventh best-selling album of all time, selling over 50 million copies.

So when it comes to *The Dark Side Of The Moon*, the main decision is which version should you go for? An original Harvest pressing from 1973 can sell for as much as £250, while the US version will see change from £20. A remaster released in 2009 by Mobile Fidelity Sound Lab is similarly priced to the US original, while the version released to celebrate the album's 30th anniversary in 2003 is a little pricier, selling for as much as £100. Alternatively, you can just pop down your local record emporium and pick up the 2016 reissue, which is highly recommended.

Despite having one of the best selling albums of all time, Pink Floyd only reached #1 once in the UK

Andrew Whittuck/Redferns/Getty Images

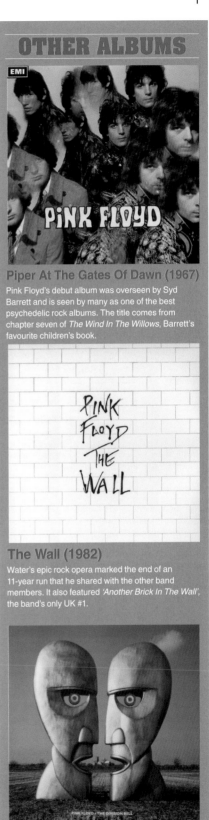

OTHER ALBUMS

EMI

Piper At The Gates Of Dawn (1967)
Pink Floyd's debut album was overseen by Syd Barrett and is seen by many as one of the best psychedelic rock albums. The title comes from chapter seven of *The Wind In The Willows*, Barrett's favourite children's book.

The Wall (1982)
Water's epic rock opera marked the end of an 11-year run that he shared with the other band members. It also featured *'Another Brick In The Wall'*, the band's only UK #1.

The Division Bell (1994)
Pink Floyd's 14th album divided critics on release, with many feeling the loss of co-founded Roger Waters. It's a real group effort however, with significant contributions from each band member. It's cover looks amazing as well.

Quadrophenia

The Who

Release Date: 1973 | Record Label: MCA

The Who were not strangers to the idea of concept albums or rock operas, experimenting with these formats on their previous records *The Who Sell Out* and *Tommy*. Entirely written by Pete Townsend, *Quadrophenia* is an album with a narrative throughout following a teenager called Jimmy, he doesn't know where he belongs in the world but then discovers the mod movement and The Who. Jimmy suffers from schizophrenia and has four personalities, hence the album title. Each of the personalities reflects a member of the band and explores a theme which reoccurs in the album. Fed up of his life at home, his dead-end job and relationships with friends and family, he moves from London to Brighton. *Quadrophenia* spoke to teens of the time and they could relate to the it.

Just like The Who's other rock opera *Tommy*, *Quahrophenia* was adapted into a film in 1973, with the same name. The adaptation of *Quadrophenia* wasn't a musical and didn't star the band. The Who play their typical grand rock that made them famous, but Townsend would add multi-tracked synthesisers as well as strings and horn parts to add to the overall sound. This would later be a hindrance to their live performance as they would

need the new instruments on backing tape, which would often malfunction and some members didn't want to be restricted by sticking to the tape. It was suggested that the band hire a fifth member to play keyboard but Roger Daltrey vetoed the idea. On the vinyl release, inside the gatefold is a summary

The Who, late '60s

of the plot of *Quadrophenia* as well as a booklet of photographs showing Brighton and London during the mod scene, when then album was set.

Track List

SIDE A
Track 1: I Am the Sea
Track 2: The Real Me
Track 3: Quadrophenia
Track 4: Cut My Hair
Track 5: The Punk and the Godfather
SIDE B
Track 1: I'm One
Track 2: The Dirty Jobs
Track 3: Helpless Dancer
Track 4: Is It in My Head?
Track 5: I've Had Enough
SIDE C
Track 1: 5:15
Track 2: Sea and Sand
Track 3: Drowned
Track 4: Bell Boy
SIDE D
Track 1: Doctor Jimmy
Track 2: The Rock
Track 3: Love, Reign o'er Me

A Night At The Opera

Queen

Release Date: 1975 | **Record Label:** EMI/Elektra

Record label EMI took an unusual gamble on *Queen with A Night At The Opera*. At the time of its release it was the most expensive album ever made and back then the quartet weren't the biggest band around. Why the record label took this risk is unknown but the gamble paid off. *A Night At The Opera* cemented Queen as a household name and, pardon the pun, music royalty. The album title came from a film by the Marx Brothers of the same name which the band watched while recording in the studio. The album features Queen's normal variety of genres as well as experimentation of sounds and recording techniques. There are tracks that are all-out rock but the band doesn't seem to

Queen, 3 September 1984

take themselves too seriously in their music. Take for example *'Seaside Rendezvous'* where Mercury imitates woodwind instruments using just his voice. However, they have the occasional serious moment such as in the opening track *'Death On Two Legs'* which is said to be a hate song directed towards Queen's original manager. *'Love Of My Life'* was written by Freddie Mercury about his then-girlfriend Mary Austin and was so popular that at live performances Mercury wouldn't sing any of the lyrics, allowing the fans to sing it. The band's guitarist Brian May would later rearrange the song and after Mercury's death, dedicate it to him when playing it live.

You can't mention a *Night At The Opera* without bringing up *'Bohemian Rhapsody'*, the best-selling commercial single of all time in the UK and one of the band's most well-known songs. It was also the most expensive single to produce at the time of its release, being recording in multiple studios and taking over three weeks to make. It was twice the length of most singles and received only mixed reviews at the time, if you can believe it. Now it is one of the most well-known rock songs of all time; it has topped charts around the world and remains to be a popular choice with drunk karaoke singers everywhere.

Track List

SIDE A

Track 1: Death On Two Legs (Dedicated To...)
Track 2: Lazing On A Sunday Afternoon
Track 3: I'm In Love With My Car
Track 4: You're My Best Friends
Track 5: '39
Track 6: Sweet Lady
Track 7: Seaside Rendezvous

SIDE B

Track 1: The Prophet's Song
Track 2: Love Of My Life
Track 3: Good Company
Track 4: Bohemian Rhapsody
Track 5: God Save The Queen

Hotel California

Eagles

Release Date: 1976 | **Record Label:** Asylum Records

"Welcome to the Hotel California." On the Eagles' fifth studio album, they conjured up the allegorical hotel as a means to convey their disillusionment with the supposed 'American dream' — just the beginning of a wider commentary on the self-destructive nature of the rock music industry at the time, the United States and the wider world. Indisputably one of the most iconic rock albums of all time, *Hotel California* won the band a Grammy Award (Record Of The Year for the album's title track) and has sold over 30 million copies (the Eagles' second highest selling album of all, after the success of *Their Greatest Hits* (1971—1975).

Hotel California marked guitarist Joe Walsh's band debut, whilst also the final LP with bassist Randy Meisner. The album was recorded at Criteria Studios, Florida and Record Plant Studios, California with producer Bill Szymczyk who had also worked on the Eagles' previous record, *One Of These Nights*. Recording sessions at Criteria Studios were often disrupted by the noise from Black Sabbath working on Technical Ecstasy in the studio next door.

The LP's artwork was intended to reflect an atmosphere of "faded glory, loss of innocence and decadence," turning to renowned British designer John Kosh (responsible for The Beatles' *Abbey Road* and The Who's *Who's Next* vinyl covers) to achieve such feelings. The opulent Beverly Hills Hotel on Sunset Boulevard was chosen as the cover's main subject, shot with the help of David Alexander at dusk from a 60-foot high cherry-picker platform.

The first pressings of *Hotel California* continues a tradition started on the group's third album, *On The Border*, of having messages etched into the run-out grooves. Side A reads "Is It 6 O'clock Yet?" and Side B features "V.O.L. Is Five-Piece Live," the latter a nod to the band's decision to record the instrumental track for '*Victim Of Love*' live.

History of the Eagles tour, 2014

Track List

SIDE A
Track 1: Hotel California
Track 2: New Kid In Town
Track 3: Life In The Fast Lane
Track 4: Wasted Time
SIDE B
Track 1: Wasted Time (Reprise)
Track 2: Victim Of Love
Track 3: Pretty Maids All In A Row
Track 4: Try And Love Again
Track 5: The Last Resort

Ramones

Ramones

Release Date: 1976 | **Record Label:** Plaza Sound Studios

Eliminate the unnecessary, and focus on the substance." Drummer Tommy Ramone's succinctly sums up no fuss attitude of the Ramones' self-titled debut, which was recorded in a single week for only $6,400. The record runs for a meager 29 minutes and each of the tracks clock in at just over two and a half minutes each.

The four-piece band are largely considered to have established the entire genre of punk rock, despite their less than stellar sales upon their album's release. The record only peaked at #111 in the US charts and the two singles subsequently released from the album ('Blitzkreig Bop' and 'I Wanna Be Your Boyfriend') failed to chart at all. In fact the album only sold a total of 6,000 copies in the entirety its first year, eventually being certified gold with half a million sales but only 38 years later.

Having made a name for themselves regularly playing shows for two years before their debut, the Ramones had over 30 songs ready to record when the entered Plaza Sound Studios with producer Craig Leon. The band felt it was essential capture the excitement and energy of their live shows, to which end they recorded the tracks in the order they'd play them live. With its insanely catchy refrain and frantic pace, 'Blitzkrieg Bop' is one the best album-openers of all time and alone reason enough to give Ramones a spin.

Initially the album's cover was to be in the style of 1964's *Meet The Beatles!*, a striking, high contrast photograph of John, Paul, George and Ringo. $2,000 was spent by Sire on a photoshoot, but ultimately the idea was scrapped after the band and record label were dissatisfied with the results. Instead a black-and-white photograph of Roberta Bayley's taken for Punk

magazine was used for Ramones' cover, featuring (from left to right) Johnny, Tommy, Joey and Dee Dee against a brick wall. The iconic photograph has since been widely imitated — Lou Reed's New York and Ultravox's eponymous debut to name a few.

Track List

SIDE A
Track 1: Blitzkrieg Bop
Track 2: Beat On The Brat
Track 3: Judy Is A Punk
Track 4: I Wanna Be Your Boyfriend
Track 5: Chain Saw
Track 6: Now I Wanna Sniff Some Glue
Track 7: I Don't Wanna Go Down To The Basement

SIDE B
Track 1: Loudmouth
Track 2: Havana Affair
Track 3: Listen To My Heart
Track 4: 53rd & 3rd
Track 5: Let's Dance
Track 6: I Don't Wanna Walk Around With You
Track 7: Today Your Love, Tomorrow The World

Ramones in 1976

Songs In The Key Of Life

Stevie Wonder

Release Date: 1976 | **Record Label:** Tamla Motown

Few albums have contained with their grooves as huge an amount of energy, creativity and sheer songwriting exuberance as *Songs In The Key Of Life*, a vast, four-sided explosion of music released by the then 26-year-old Stevie Wonder. The songwriter's best-selling and best-known album, at least from his classic '70s period, *Songs* wasn't merely a collection of compositions — it was a critique of America as it was in 1976 and a turning-point in the history of soul music.

The album's background was fairly chaotic, which perhaps goes some way to explaining the feeling of expressive energy which it gives off. Wonder had been seriously considering retirement from the music industry, although he was riding a wave of huge commercial and critical approval after three hit albums — *Talking Book*, *Innervisions* and *Fulfillingness' First Finale*, released between 1972 and '74. Angered by the American government and contemplating a move to Ghana, he was persuaded to continue with his career as a musician when a new, record-breaking contract with Motown was presented to him. The new deal, a seven-year agreement worth $37 million and the largest ever signed at the time, guaranteed Wonder full artistic control.

In this context, it's no surprise that Wonder decided to forge ahead with his grand vision. Presented with an artistic platform of such scope, he was able to embark on a songwriting and recording spree that took up two years of his life and an enormous amount of creative energy. It was reported that Wonder would work for days on end without sleep or food, consumed by the enormous wave of inspiration that flooded over him.

The results, released after a long delay taken up by extra remixing, were astounding. The album contained no fewer than 17 songs, plus four more which were shoehorned onto an accompanying EP, curiously titled *A Something's Extra*. Instrumental passages of great complexity abounded (see *'Contusion'*), interspersed with perfect pop singles

Track List

SIDE A
Track 1: Love's In Need Of Love Today
Track 2: Have A Talk With God
Track 3: Village Ghetto Land
Track 4: Contusion
Track 5: Sir Duke

SIDE B
Track 1: I Wish
Track 2: Knocks Me Off My Feet
Track 3: Pastime Paradise
Track 4: Summer Soft
Track 5: Ordinary Pain

SIDE C
Track 1: Isn't She Lovely
Track 2: Joy Inside My Tears
Track 3: Black Man

SIDE D
Track 1: Ngiculela — Es Una Historia — I Am Singing
Track 2: If It's Magic
Track 3: As
Track 4: Another Star

A Something's Extra
(bonus EP included with special edition of album)

SIDE A
Track 1: Saturn
Track 2: Ebony Eyes

SIDE B
Track 1: All Day Sucker
Track 2: Easy Goin' Evening (My Mama's Call)

('*Sir Duke*', '*Isn't She Lovely*') and smooth funk suites ('*As*') that have been endlessly sampled in the following decades.

Viewed from four decades' distance, the sheer magnitude of *Songs In The Key Of Life* is perhaps its most lasting impression. A total of 130 musicians and studio personnel worked on it, with Wonder steering the ship with great charisma: among these were Herbie Hancock, who played Fender Rhodes; ace bassist Nate Watts, whose incredibly dexterous playing through '*Sir Duke*' and elsewhere gave the album huge presence; guitar legend George Benson; and singer Minnie Riperton.

The songs' subject matter was also cause for celebration. In '*Black Man*' and '*Ngiculela — Es Una Historia — I Am Singing*', Wonder discussed race, a touchy subject in America then as now. At the same time, he wrote love songs and peace anthems reminiscent of the hippie period of a decade before, rather than the more cynical mid-'70s. Remember, punk rock was just around the corner in '76, and supporters of that sound would argue that expansive albums such as this one were the reason for its arrival — and yet Songs went on to sell over 10 million copies in the USA alone, making it that rarest of records: a diamond-rated album. Clearly Wonder had touched a nerve among the record-buying public, not just among soul and R&B audiences but in the popular consciousness.

"Wonder would work for days on end without sleep or food, consumed by the enormous wave of inspiration"

Alongside Fleetwood Mac's *Rumours*, Pink Floyd's *Dark Side Of The Moon* and Mike Oldfield's *Tubular Bells*, all released a few years before or after *Songs In The Key Of Life*, this record became a must-buy throughout the Western world. Its immediately recognisable orange sleeve was seen on coffee tables across five continents, and like the aforementioned albums, it is difficult to imagine a recording of similar ambition being created today, let alone reaching as huge an audience.

Has the music aged well? Some of the more naive love songs are showing their age a little these days, but as a demonstration of what can happen when a genius is allowed untrammelled expression, the triumph of both Stevie Wonder and *Songs In The Key Of Life* really is undeniable.

Wonder nearly moved from the US to Ghana until he signed his creatively-free contract

OTHER ALBUMS

Signed, Sealed & Delivered (1970)
20-years-old and with a newly mature voice, Wonder delivered this infectiously compelling set of originals and covers at a time when classically optimistic Motown songwriting was about to be replaced by more socially-aware music.

Talking Book (1972)
Opening his best-known period of creativity with this album, Wonder explored new areas of thought with the lyrics of funky tunes such as '*Superstition*' and '*You Are The Sunshine Of My Life*'. It was time for the boy to become a man.

Innervisions (1973)
Wonder's most acclaimed record after Songs... itself, Innervisions takes a giant leap forward in songwriting and musicality. The great man shines brightest on '*Too High*' and '*Living In The City*', both critiques of life in '70s America.

Exodus

Bob Marley & The Wailers

Release Date: 1977 | **Record Label:** Island

More than 35 years on from his untimely death, Bob Marley remains as inescapable a presence as he ever was. His face and words have become culturally ubiquitous, memetic and recognisable everywhere from Kingston to Tokyo, and for many he still represents the personification of Jamaica. The *idea* of Bob Marley resonates so profoundly around the world that occasionally his status as one of the last century's most influential musicians can feel secondary.

It shouldn't. For all Marley's status as an icon of the 20th century, a symbol of Jamaica and proponent of Rastafarianism, he was and is, first and foremost, the man who brought reggae to the world. Of the string of seminal records that he released as Bob Marley and the Wailers across a prolific career, *Exodus* stands out. And not only for its success or longevity — its initial UK chart run lasted over a year. Had it never cracked a chart anywhere, *Exodus* could still lay claim to being the smoothest reggae record ever laid down. It's both sensual and spiritual (and frequently both), and Marley's indelible force of personality exudes wisdom, empathy and straight-up passion on every track.

Exodus is also the most hit-heavy studio record that Marley and the Wailers ever released. Side two alone is a string of seminal reggae anthems, from '*Jamming*' through to '*One Love*' via '*Waiting In Vain*' and '*Three Little Birds*'. Just one or two of these songs would be enough to elevate almost any album to classic status — that Marley nonchalantly reels them off one after the other here is near-divine.

Legend is often seen as the quintessential Marley record, but while it's difficult to argue with its dazzling, greatest-hits track list, it is still ultimately a compilation, released three years after his passing. In part, that's why you find *Exodus* on this list instead. Despite, or perhaps even because of a few minor imperfections, it's the real definitive Marley album, the fully realised work of a genius at the peak of his musical talent and powers.

Bob Marley and the Wailers perform at the Uptown Theater, Chicago, Illinois, November 1979

Track List

SIDE A

Track 1: Natural Mystic
Track 2: So Much Things to Say
Track 3: Guiltiness
Track 4: The Heathen
Track 5: Exodus

SIDE B

Track 1: Jamming
Track 2: Waiting In Vain
Track 3: Turn Your Lights Down Low
Track 4: Three Little Birds
Track 5: One Love/People Get Ready

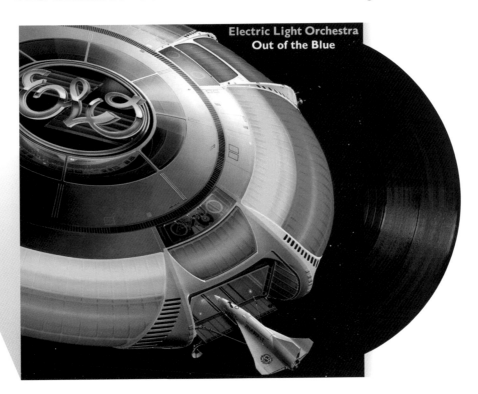

Electric Light Orchestra
Out of the Blue

Out Of The Blue

Electric Light Orchestra

Release Date: 1977 | **Record Label:** Jet/United Artists/CBS

Has there ever been a more unabashedly joyful song committed to vinyl than 'Mr. Blue Sky'? The euphoric high point of Electric Light Orchestra's (ELO's) seventh studio album, *Out Of The Blue*, has become synonymous with carefree exuberance — the official soundtrack to workers skipping out of the office on a sunny Friday afternoon. That it arrives, in all its jaunty piano, squiggly guitar and vocoded glory, at the conclusion of an internal four-song suite named *Concerto for a Rainy Day*, is indicative of the flamboyant excess of ELO mastermind Jeff Lynne's essential work.

Across four sides and more than 70 minutes, *Out Of The Blue* takes infectious pop numbers and embellishes them with every tool and instrument available in Lynne's vast production arsenal. From the layered choral grooves of *'Sweet Talkin'* Woman' to the sweeping string arrangements of *'Standin' In The Rain'*, each track is imbued with a symphonic quality. Lynne's songwriting and instrumental experimentation are given free reign, and the result is an album that's both sonically ambitious and fabulously immediate.

Never content with merely elevating its brand of rock to orchestral, ELO doubled down on its extra-terrestrial aesthetic. And this is partly why *Out Of The Blue*, more than most records, seems especially suited to vinyl, its glowing spaceship-adorned cover too expansive and ostentatious to be squeezed into the confines of a CD jewel case.

The multi-coloured doughnut was, by 1977, an integral part of the band's iconography, with Lynne and company performing their live shows from under the flashing hull of an impressive replica, and the LP's striking packaging matches the grand scale of its music. Shusei Nagaoka's dazzling illustration work is front and centre, but open the package and you'll find a DIY cardboard rendition of the good ship ELO to assemble. Try glancing up at your miniature rainbow bagel as *'Turn To Stone'* begins to play without smiling.

Track List

SIDE A
Track 1: Turn To Stone
Track 2: It's Over
Track 3: Sweet Talkin' Woman
Track 4: Across The Border

SIDE B
Track 1: Night In The City
Track 2: Starlight
Track 3: Jungle
Track 4: Believe Me Now
Track 5: Steppin' Out

SIDE C (Concerto For A Rainy Day)
Track 1: Standin' In The Rain
Track 2: Big Wheels
Track 3: Summer And Lightning
Track 4: Mr. Blue Sky

SIDE D
Track 1: Sweet Is The Night
Track 2: The Whale
Track 3: Birmingham Blues
Track 4: Wild West Hero

Electric Light Orchestra
1977 Lineup

Rumours

Fleetwood Mac

Release Date: 1977 | **Record Label:** Warner Bros.

On its 11th record, Fleetwood Mac crafted a bittersweet masterpiece fuelled by perhaps one of rock's most infamous melodramas. Released in 1977, the intensely personal *Rumours* has become the seventh highest-selling studio album of all time with over 45 million copies sold worldwide. Also winning the five-piece a Grammy award for Album Of The Year in 1978, the iconic record not only features Fleetwood Mac's best work but some of the best songwriting of all time.

The seminal LP featured the fifth incarnation of the band - the duo of guitarist Lindsey Buckingham and vocalist Stevie Nicks joining Mick Fleetwood, Christine McVie and John McVie two years previous following the departure of Bob Welch. A transition triggered on 1975's eponymous release, *Rumours* completes Fleetwood Mac's progression from a band of blues cliches to one of bright pop singles and immaculate songwriting.

Inescapably intrinsic to *Rumours*, the romantic turmoil plaguing the band during its creation has

been well documented. Christine and John McVie were going through a divorce after eight years of marriage; Buckingham and Nicks were going through a breakup, ending their on/off relationship; Fleetwood had discovered that his wife was having an affair with his best friend; and to deal with their respective personal dramas, Nicks and Fleetwood had their own affair. All of this was compounded further by inaccurate press reports and circling, ahem, rumours. The saga surrounding the recording of the album lead to the brutally honest and excruciatingly emotional love songs, which dominate the track listing.

Rumours' working title during early recording sessions was *'Yesterday's Gone'*, taken from the chorus of *'Don't Stop'*. The majority of the recording was done at Record Plant Studios in Sausalito, California, with producers Ken Caillat and Richard Dashut, though Fleetwood and John McVie retained ultimate creative control. Later recording was moved to various studios around Los Angeles, including Wally Heider Studios. Stories of Fleetwood Mac's pursuit of sonic perfection in

> **"The romantic turmoil plaguing the band during [Rumours'] creation has been well documented"**

Track List

SIDE A
Track 1:	Second Hand News
Track 2:	Dreams
Track 3:	Never Going Back Again
Track 4:	Don't Stop
Track 5:	Go Your Own Way
Track 6:	Songbird

SIDE B
Track 1:	The Chain
Track 2:	You Make Loving Fun
Track 3:	I Don't Want to Know
Track 4:	Oh Daddy
Track 5:	Gold Dust Woman

the studio are infamous — Buckingham's acoustic guitar was restrung every 20 minutes while recording *'Never Going Back Again'* to achieve the same bright sound of a fresh set of strings on every take. And during sessions for *'The Chain'*, five days were spent producing the perfect drum sound for Fleetwood.

Songwriting duties were mainly shared between the vocal trio of Nicks (*'Dreams'*, *'I Don't Wanna Know'*, *'Gold Dust Woman'*), Buckingham (*'Second Hand News'*, *'Never Going Back Again'*, *'Go Your Own Way'*) and Christine McVie (*'Don't Stop'*, *'Songbird'*, *'You Make Loving Fun'*, *'Oh Daddy'*). While at its core is an unfinished track by Christine McVie written a year earlier, *'The Chain'* is the only track on the record credited to all five members of Fleetwood Mac. After using McVie's *'Keep Me There'* as a starting point, Buckingham borrowed a guitar section from a track he recorded with Nicks in 1973 called *'Lola (My Love)'*. Nicks contributed lyrics to the track later in the album's production.

Rumours' cover, featuring Fleetwood and Nicks (as her on stage persona, Rhiannon) was the result of a joint effort by photographer Herbert Worthington,

and designers Desmond Strobel and Larry Vigon. A curious detail of the cover, the wooden balls (actually, toilet chains) hanging from Fleetwood's crotch actually continue a long-running gag. After ripping them off the toilets in a club after a gig, the drummer began to wear the lavatory chains dangling between his legs during the band's performances and eventually they became a good-luck charm of sorts. The LP was accompanied by a printed gatefold insert featuring lyrics and a collage of band photos. Some original pressings of the record also feature a textured sleeve.

Unfortunately not making the cut on the original track listing due to the constraints of '70s vinyl pressing, Nicks' *'Silver Springs'* (which was unsurprisingly written about Buckingham) featured on later reissues and became somewhat of a cult favourite with fans. Among the plethora of official and unofficial rereleases over the past 40 years, audiophiles will revel in the 2011 version that was released for US Record Store Day, which was cut at 45rpm on heavyweight 180g vinyl and remastered from the original analogue tapes to achieve maximum audio quality.

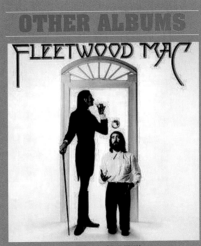

OTHER ALBUMS

Fleetwood Mac (1977)

Recorded at the beginning of the Buckingham/Nicks era. Featuring Nicks' classic *Rhiannon*, the self-titled record took almost a year to climb to the top of the charts.

Tusk (1979)

The most expensive rock record to date when it was released in 1979. The double LP heralds the start of an experimental streak following *Rumours'* overwhelming success.

The Dance (1997)

Reuniting the *Rumours*-era lineup for the first time in a decade, this live album plays as a greatest-hits album. Rumours offcut *Silver Springs* receives a notable outing.

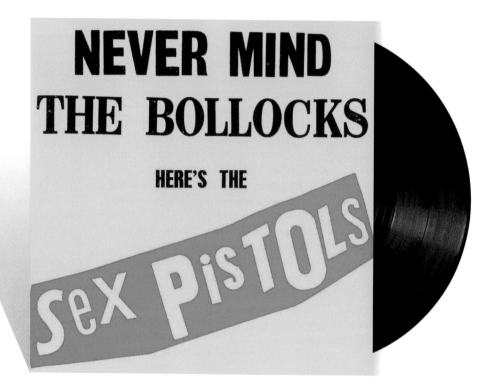

Never Mind The Bollocks Here's The Sex Pistols

Sex Pistols

Release Date: 1977 | Record Label: Virgin

Looking back, it's remarkable how little actual music the Sex Pistols made in their fleeting first run from 1975 to 1978. The band that catapulted the UK punk scene from bubbling counter-culture sideshow to bona fide musical revolution had just a handful of singles and a sole studio album to their name by the time they walked offstage for the final time at the Winterland Ballroom in San Francisco. The band's antics, their infamy, and their influence on a generation of punk bands that would follow are disproportionately vast when compared with their output. But then, if you're only going to make one record, it might as well be one that changes the world.

Never Mind The Bollocks did exactly that. Arriving on the crest of a wave of publicity and scandal, its anarchic and unrefined sound was a rejection of the mainstream music peddled and consumed by the loathsome establishment. Listening now, Johnny Rotten's leering vocals still seethe with disdain, irreverence and a barely contained violence, while the ragged guitar and propulsive percussion eschew any sort of nuance or subtlety in favour of sticking two middle fingers up at conventional, mannered rock and roll.

The production is rough, and bassist Sid Vicious' musical talent was famously lacking (indeed, aside from *'Bodies'*, *Never Mind…'s* basslines were all recorded by guitarist Steve Jones). But these streaks do nothing to dull the album's caustic appeal. Its edges just mean that the Sex Pistols' vitriol cuts even deeper.

There have been reissues, remasters, demo collections and the occasional live recording repackaged and flogged over the last few decades. And the band has performed — in its original, pre-Vicious form — on a number of occasions since their Filthy Lucre reunion tour in 1996. But none of this music has the same power or vitality as *Never Mind The Bollocks* in its original form. It's lightning in a bottle stuff, thrilling as ever, and impossible to replicate.

Track List

SIDE A
Track 1: Holidays In The Sun
Track 2: Bodies
Track 3: No Feelings
Track 4: Liar
Track 5: Problems
Track 6: God Save The Queen

SIDE B
Track 1: Seventeen
Track 2: Anarchy In The UK
Track 3: Sub-Mission
Track 4: Pretty Vacant
Track 5: New York
Track 6: EMI

Jorgen Angel/Redferns, Chris Walter/WireImage

Aja
Steely Dan

Release Date: 1977 | **Record Label:** ABC

Elsewhere in this book you'll read about *The Epic*, an album recorded by jazz saxophonist Kamasi Washington in 2015. Beloved by critics but only bought by a few thousand fans of jazz-rock, a niche musical genre these days, we bring it up here because its fate — to be respected but barely heard — is exactly what would have befallen *Aja*, Steely Dan's sixth album, had that now 40-year-old LP been released today. And yet Aja has sold five million copies, is in the Grammy Hall of Fame and regularly appears in Top 100 Albums lists. How times have changed, eh?

Still, *Aja* deserves every bit of its acclaim. Steely Dan were and remain a duo comprising two multi-

instrumentalists, Donald Fagen and Walter Becker, and between these two prodigious talents all of the rock, jazz and soul worlds were covered. It helped that the backing musicians were the very cream of the Los Angeles session world, including guitarist Lee Ritenour, bassist Chuck Rainey, drummer Steve Gadd and saxophonist Wayne Shorter, but the album wouldn't have reached such a wide audience without excellent songs at its core.

This makes it all the more fascinating that Aja isn't a double album, as you'd expect with this much talent stuffed into it, or indeed a particularly long single LP. *Aja* only has seven songs, in fact, but each is a gem, from *'Peg'* — one of Steely Dan's best-known songs — through to the title cut, Josie and Deacon Blues (whose title inspired the name of a certain Scottish band from the '80s).

Many decades later, Aja has aged both well and less well. The glistening production job, a precision-engineered treatment which bagged its own Grammy award and which is an object lesson to this day in how to make music sound good, still feels fantastic. The songs, however, may be a little smooth for anyone looking for adrenalised thrills: Fagen and Becker specialised in catchy, slick textures that soothed rather than stimulated, so don't expect too many sudden left turns.

Track List

SIDE A
Track 1: Black Cow
Track 2: Aja
Track 3: Deacon Blues
SIDE B
Track 1: Peg
Track 2: Home At Last
Track 3: I Got The News
Track 4: Josie

Donald Fagen of Steely Dan

Steely Dan, 1977

Chris Walter/WireImage.

Live And Dangerous

Thin Lizzy

Release Date: 1973 | **Record Label:** Vertigo

Thin Lizzy, the hard rock titans fronted by the iconic Irish singer Phil Lynott, had already released seven albums in six years by the time they got around to releasing a live collection — but when it came, it was a monster. A double album of live tunes recorded in various locations, *Live And Dangerous* was one of the earliest in-concert collection to match, or even surpass, the studio skills of the band which created it. Some of this, it has long been known, was the result of some judicious overdubbing in the studio after the live recordings — although to what extent this took place, and by whom, has been the subject of varying accounts.

Masterminded by producer Tony Visconti, whose track record with David Bowie, T-Rex and other artists had made him something of a king among his profession, the album pulls off the trick of sounding both live and polished. Lynott's laddish stage presence is made evident in between-song statements such as "Is there anyone here with any Irish in them... and would any of the gals like any more Irish in them?" and guitar fans gasped at the famous harmony solos delivered by Scott Gorham and Brian Robertson.

'Rosalie' was the single released from the LP,

but frankly any number of songs represent its sheer energy equally well — not least the opening cut, *'Jailbreak'*, and a furious take on what is arguably Lizzy's most famous song, *'The Boys Are Back In Town'*. The textures of their live material were improved no end by a sax player, John Earle, and none other than Huey Lewis — yes, that infamous Huey Lewis, himself still five years away from global success.

Like Motorhead's *No Sleep 'Til Hammersmith*, released three years later, *Live And Dangerous* remains one of the quintessential live albums of the golden age of hard rock. Lynott may have succumbed to his lifestyle seven years later, but his legacy as a live performer is secure.

Thin Lizzy's live performances were legendary

Track List

SIDE A
Track 1: Jailbreak
Track 2: Emerald
Track 3: Southbound
Track 4: Rosalie/Cowgirl's Song

SIDE B
Track 1: Dancing In The Moonlight (It's Caught Me In Its Spotlight)
Track 2: Massacre
Track 3: Still In Love With You
Track 4: Johnny The Fox Meets Jimmy The Weed

SIDE C
Track 1: Cowboy Song
Track 2: The Boys Are Back In Town
Track 3: Don't Believe A Word
Track 4: Warriors
Track 5: Are You Ready

SIDE D
Track 1: Suicide
Track 2: Sha La La
Track 3: Baby Drives Me Crazy
Track 4: The Rocker

Armed Forces

Elvis Costello

Release Date: 1979 | **Record Label:** Radar Records

The timing of Irish songwriter Elvis Costello's third album, Armed Forces, could not have been better when it appeared in 1979. Punk rock was waning, but its fans liked Costello's snappy guitar riffs and lyrical edge; mod was in the middle of a resurgence, and with his glasses, skinny tie and preppy look, he fitted

Armed Forces struck a cord with many rock listeners

that image perfectly; and an appreciation of politically astute, melodic songs that came and went quickly was in the air. Somehow, Costello suited the times perfectly.

It helped, of course, that *Armed Forces* was packed full of killer songs. The obvious hit, and indeed the song for which Costello remains best known to this day, was *'Oliver's Army'*. Although the singer has never explained with much clarity what the song is about — whether it's Oliver Cromwell or Winston Churchill — its barbed references to South Africa (then languishing in apartheid stasis) and even *"a white n****"* seemed to be politically critical at a time when such criticism was sorely needed. Musically, the song was joyous: its intro, composed of multiple pianos chiming in perfect unison, is instantly thrilling, and credit should go both to Costello's backing band The Attractions and the album's producer Nick Lowe, himself a somewhat legendary songwriter.

The other big hit from *Armed Forces* was *'Accidents Will Happen'*, a showcase for the more downbeat side of Costello's songwriting as well as his unique singing voice, a kind of adenoidal croon. Elsewhere on the album, the singer pulls no punches on songs such as *'Two Little Hitlers'*, and revealed the character of a bitter lover spurned on *'Moods For Moderns'*. As he sang the line *"Soon you'll belong to someone else/And I will be your stranger just pretending"*, you

felt his emotion, even though it wasn't quite clear what that emotion might be. Whatever the message of this obscure album, it struck home with a huge demographic of rock listeners, who promptly sent it to #2 on the UK albums chart.

Track List

SIDE A
Track 1: Accidents Will Happen
Track 2: Senior Service
Track 3: Oliver's Army
Track 4: Big Boys
Track 5: Green Shirt
Track 6: Party Girl
SIDE B
Track 1: Goon Squad
Track 2: Busy Bodies
Track 3: Moods For Moderns
Track 4: Chemistry Class
Track 5: Two Little Hitlers
Track 6: (What's So Funny 'Bout) Peace, Love And Understanding

Unknown Pleasures

Joy Division

Release Date: 1979 | **Record Label:** Factory Records

Whilst met with a decidedly mixed response following its initial release in 1979, Unknown Pleasures has since become an album of regular critical acclaim. The album's status as a cornerstone of the post-punk genre is irrefutable and under producer Martin Hannett, the four-piece established the unmistakable Joy Division sound on their 39-minute debut LP — propulsive punk driven by lead singer Ian Curtis' anguish. Less than a year after the record's release Curtis committed suicide at the age of 23, further compounding the poignancy of his lyrics.

Hannett employed an array of unorthodox techniques during the album's production, such as recording Curtis' vocals for *'Insight'* through a telephone line. Bottles smashing, someone eating crisps and a basement toilet were amongst some of the sound effects used, as well as the Powertran Transcendent 2000 synthesiser of which so much of the LP's identity is owed. It cost £18,000 to produce over the course of three weekends at Stockport's Strawberry Studios, and became a catalyst for future successes for Factory Records.

Unknown Pleasures is fronted by one of the most iconic of album covers and perhaps alone is reason enough to own this record — Peter Saville's understated design, which depicts 100 successive pulses from the first discovered pulsar, printed in the centre of a black, textured sleeve. The enigmatic diagram, originally found in The Cambridge Encyclopaedia of Astronomy, has since transcended the record's art and has since been re-created or parodied on everything from T-shirts to condom wrappers. The original pressing of 10,000 copies also features the groove notations *'This is the way'* on Side A (*'Outside'*) and *'Step'* on Side B (*'Inside'*) — both prominent lyrics taken from *'Atrocity Exhibition'*, the opening track of the band's follow-up album, *Closer*. No singles were released from the album and, against the norm, Joy Division didn't include lyrics with the record.

Track List

SIDE A
Track 1: Disorder
Track 2: Day Of The Lords
Track 3: Candidate
Track 4: Insight
Track 5: New Dawn Fades
SIDE B
Track 1: She's Lost Control
Track 2: Shadowplay
Track 3: Wilderness
Track 4: Interzone
Track 5: I Remember Nothing

Joy Division - Bernard Sumner, Stephen Morris, Ian Curtis, Peter Hook performing live onstage at Bowdon Vale Youth Club

London Calling

The Clash

Release Date: 1979 | **Record Label:** CBS

A double album is all too often synonymous with self-indulgence or a lack of creative discipline. In the final few weeks of the '70s The Clash released their third album *London Calling*, a 19-track double album which is neither of the above. And, at only the cost of a standard single LP release, it was a bargain. The record's lyrics tackle a multitude of social and political issues, such as social displacement, racial conflict, unemployment and drug. Owing to each band member's individual influences, *London Calling* also

expertly blends a range of musical styles, including reggae, ska, jazz, rockabilly and pop to name a few. Frontman Joe Strummer once mused that one of the things that makes The Clash so great was that all four of them contributed something different — that's certainly true here and it shows, displaying the confidence and craft of a band in their prime.

Pennie Smith took the cover photograph of bassist Paul Simonon smashing his Fender Precision bass (the remains which are now on display at the Cleveland Rock and Roll Hall of Fame) on stage at The Palladium in New York. Smith wasn't keen on the photo but the band, along with their graphic designer Rob Lowry, decided to use it anyway. In a nod to Elvis Presley's self-titled debut album, Lowry added the distinctive pink and green lettering.

Whilst the band always planned for *London Calling* to be produced as a double LP, their record label, CBS, were resistant to the idea and insisted instead on a bonus 12-inch single. This ultimately became a full second LP. Original copies also included a printed inner sleeve, featuring lyrics and photos of the band.

The album's final track, '*Train in Vain*', was excluded from the LP's track listing on first pressings, planned instead to be given away through a promotion with NME. This deal fell through and the track was added to the album at the last minute.

Track List

SIDE A
Track 1: London Calling
Track 2: Brand New Cadillac
Track 3: Jimmy Jazz
Track 4: Hateful
Track 5: Rudie Can't Fail

SIDE B
Track 1: Spanish Bombs
Track 2: The Right Profile
Track 3: Lost In The Supermarket
Track 4: Clampdown
Track 5: The Guns Of Brixton

SIDE C
Track 1: Wrong 'Em Boyo
Track 2: Death Or Glory
Track 3: Koka Kola
Track 4: The Card Cheat

SIDE D
Track 1: Lover's Rock
Track 2: Four Horsemen
Track 3: I'm Not Down
Track 4: Revolution Rock
Track 5: Train In Vain

The Specials

The Specials

Release Date: 1979 | **Record Label:** 2 Tone Records

How do you capture lightning in a bottle, musically speaking? Well, in the case of the Specials' immortal first album, all the necessary ingredients happened to be in place. There was a cool producer at the top of his game, in this case Elvis Costello; a killer record label run more on enthusiasm than expertise, 2 Tone; an iconic monochrome checkerboard art direction; and a multiracial cast of musicians which simply could not be bettered.

Ska fans will know the line-up by heart: vocalist Terry Hall, one of British music's most enduring personalities; his fellow singer Neville Staple; guitarists Lynval Golding and Roderick 'Roddy Radiation' Byers; legendary bassist Horace Staples, aka Sir Horace Gentleman; drummer John Bradbury; and keyboardist Jerry Dammers, also the owner of 2 Tone.

Full of vitriol and musical skill, this unique line-up hit gold on their first album, released in 1979. Unusually for such a reggae-influenced band, the tempos were often medium to upbeat — see the phenomenal *'Too Much Too Young'*, later the title of a Specials compilation — which helped pull in a rock crowd to the gigs. The band shared the concerns of its audience, listing the IRA, UDA and other newsworthy organisations of the day in *'Do The Dog'*, while the sentiments of *'Concrete Jungle'* spoke volumes to the urban youth of the late '70s.

Most of all, the almost insanely funky bass-lines of songs such as *'Little Bitch'* made an entire generation of kids want to pogo up and down in moshpits, as no-one called them back then: little wonder that punks and mods alike loved the Specials. The genius ran through this album like writing in a stick of rock: *'Doesn't Make It Alright'* was another groove-heavy song, this time one which called for awareness of street violence. Nite Klub — featuring vocals from star-in-waiting Pretenders singer Chrissie Hynde — featured the maddeningly infectious off-beat guitar and organ chords which most readily identified the ska sound. A cover of Toots Hibbert's *'Monkey Man'* proved that

> **"This album had come to occupy such an embedded place in British musical culture"**

Track List

SIDE A
- **Track 1:** A Message To You Rudy
- **Track 2:** Do The Dog
- **Track 3:** It's Up To You
- **Track 4:** Nite Klub
- **Track 5:** Doesn't Make It Alright
- **Track 6:** Concrete Jungle
- **Track 7:** Too Hot

SIDE B
- **Track 1:** Monkey Man
- **Track 2:** (Dawning Of A) New Era
- **Track 3:** Blank Expression
- **Track 4:** Stupid Marriage
- **Track 5:** Too Much Too Young
- **Track 6:** Little Bitch
- **Track 7:** You're Wondering Now

The Specials on stage in Chicago, Illinois, 2013

the Specials could nail the original roots style when they wanted to, injecting the original classic with a ton of energy.

By the time of its reissue in 2002, this album had come to occupy such an embedded place in British musical culture that its subversive nature was less obvious. Considered in more depth, though, its significance became clear. In the era of race riots in London and Liverpool, a multiracial band hitting the top of the charts really meant something. Then there was the Specials' amping-up of traditionally mellow black music into an amalgam of rock and ska that — crucially — appropriated nothing: no-one saw that achievement coming in 1979.

In the same context, it should be noted that Madness — fellow Londoners who infused a similar, but not identical, musical formula with pop choruses and sold millions of albums — somehow outdid The Specials, at least commercially. The two bands shared a fanbase, and continued to do so while the Specials later morphed into the Special AKA and then fell into only sporadic activity. Between the two acts, an awareness of black music was engendered in the consciousness of white British kids that a decade of roots Jamaican music had not instilled.

That speaks volumes about the power of the songs here.

It's also interesting to note that the trajectory of the original Specials was brief but bright. After this album and a follow-up called *More Specials* in 1980, the band began to fragment after their biggest hit, a single in '81 called *'Ghost Town'*. Haunting and funky in equal measure, the song summed up the group's critical approach to British life at the time.

A footnote about the Specials' influence in America. If you recall any of the ska-punk bands of the '90s and '00s — No Doubt and The Mighty Mighty Bosstones among them — you'll hear how much of a chord they struck on that continent. Ska's rebellious nature appealed to American kids just as it did over here.

The group were critical to British life

OTHER ALBUMS

More Specials (1980)

More Specials is the second-best album by this fiery band, loaded with killer cuts from *'Rat Race'* — its biggest hit — on down. This time around, there were lounge sounds aplenty as well as the usual razor-sharp dub and reggae influences.

Today's Specials (1996)

Sure, the reformed Specials may not have found their '80s niche too readily when they got back together in the mid-'90s, but that doesn't mean this album should be discounted. This version of the band had plenty to going for it.

Guilty 'Til Proved Innocent! (1998)

A relief from the diet of cover versions in which the recent version of The Specials specialised, this album of original material proved that the old boys of ska still had what it took. Neville Staple and Horace Panter were the driving force.

'80s

Back In Black

AC/DC

Release Date: 1980 | Record Label: Albert/Atlantic

In 1980 AC/DC looked to be on their way up, they had released a series of successful records, finally broke in the US with their album *Highway To Hell* and the band was set to record what would become *Back In Black*. However in February 1980 the band's original singer Bon Scott was found dead in his friend's car after binge drinking at a club in London. After Scott's funeral, and some encouragement from his parents, the band went straight to finding a new frontman. They auditioned a number of vocalists including then-Slade singer Noddy Holder. Brian Johnson was announced as the new singer for AC/DC in April 1980, the group looked for a vocalist who wouldn't copy Scott's style, and out of respect to the deceased singer they didn't use any of the lyrics he wrote for *Back In Black* as they felt it would be like they were cashing in on his death. Much of the music was written during studio sessions while Scott was alive, fans can only imagine how it would have turned out if the he had not passed away.

Shortly after announcing the new singer to the

> **"The band pay tribute to their former singer with the album's black cover"**

public, the band set off to record in the Bahamas, but they were met with rough weather, regular tropical storms caused power cuts at the studio. But this did influence the opening lyrics to the album: *"I'm rolling thunder pouring rain, I'm coming on like a hurricane, my lightning's flashing across the sky, you're only young, but you're gonna die."* The band pay tribute to their former singer with the album's black cover, it was meant to be entirely black with embossed lettering but the record label insisted on including grey for the band's logo. The album also starts with bells ringing for Bon Scott. Apart from that brief opening, there are no reflective, mourning or sad songs. In general, the band stuck with what they knew: simple, hard-hitting rock and roll.

Back In Black is full of riffs that every novice guitar player will attempt to learn at least once, and has solos that experienced players wish they could emulate. Songs like *'You Shook Me All Night Long'* have infection choruses that suit the massive arenas they would eventually fill, and *'Shoot to Thrill'* is an adrenaline-filled rock anthem that would be used on film soundtracks years after

Track List

SIDE A
Track 1: Hells Bells
Track 2: Shoot To Thrill
Track 3: What Do You Do For Money Honey
Track 4: Given The Dog A Bone
Track 5: Let Me Put My Love Into You
SIDE B
Track 1: Back In Black
Track 2: You Shook Me All Night Long
Track 3: Have A Drink On Me
Track 4: Shake A Leg
Track 5: Rock And Roll Ain't Noise Pollution

its release. What fans would be critiquing more than anything was how well Brian Johnson performed on the album. Producer Robert Lange knew this so he demanded perfection during the recording. Whether he was superior to Bon Scott is up for debate, but Johnson's voice suited the band, his screams were passionate and he could write memorable lyrics. *Back In Black's* catchy riffs and quotable lyrics are so synonymous with rock music that they are known by even the casual listener and are still staples in AC/DC's live performances to this day.

Released in July 1980, the album is still the second best-selling album of all time. Despite selling so many records, *Back In Black* didn't reach #1 in the US. On its initial release it would only reach #4 in the charts across the pond, but did reach #1 in the UK, their home country, Australia, and France. Each time the album has been reissued, and reached the Billboards charts again, it has only managed to reach #1 on the Billboard Top Pop Catalogue.

Fans may disagree on who is the better singer, Bon Scott or Brian Johnson, but they can agree that *Back In Black* is the best AC/DC album.

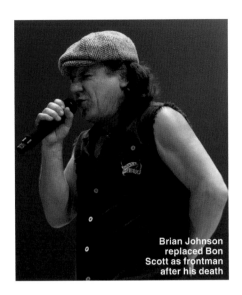

Brian Johnson replaced Bon Scott as frontman after his death

Guitarist Angus Young is the only original member left in the band's line up

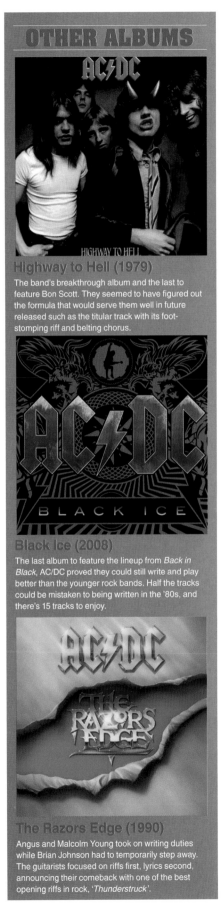

OTHER ALBUMS

Highway to Hell (1979)

The band's breakthrough album and the last to feature Bon Scott. They seemed to have figured out the formula that would serve them well in future released such as the titular track with its foot-stomping riff and belting chorus.

Black Ice (2008)

The last album to feature the lineup from *Back in Black*, AC/DC proved they could still write and play better than the younger rock bands. Half the tracks could be mistaken to being written in the '80s, and there's 15 tracks to enjoy.

The Razors Edge (1990)

Angus and Malcolm Young took on writing duties while Brian Johnson had to temporarily step away. The guitarists focused on riffs first, lyrics second, announcing their comeback with one of the best opening riffs in rock, '*Thunderstruck*'.

Sound Affects

The Jam

Release Date: 1980 | **Record Label:** Polydor

The Jam released six studio albums between 1977 and 1982; of these, *Sound Affects* was the fifth, and singer Paul Weller's favourite. The reasons for this seem obvious to any fan of this pioneering London trio: the album is razor-sharp but well-produced; ambitious while never straying too far from pop/mod focus; and without the intra-band tensions that made its follow-up, *The Gift*, the sound of a band in flux. What's most astounding, now that Weller is no fewer than 13 albums into a successful post-Jam career, is that he made those six Jam albums between the ages of 19 and 24. That's a youth well-spent, if you ask us. As a result, there's plenty of youthful bile on this album, of course. Weller and his compadres Bruce Foxton (bass) and Rick Buckler (drums) fitted in perfectly with the punk-rock movement, critical as they were of the establishment and confrontational in image. Clad in the latest revivalist mod threads, the Jam and the punk kids got on famously — after all, what is a punk but a mod with safety pins?

And if you're still not sure who bought all those copies of *Sound Affects*, listen to the sardonic *'That's Entertainment'* (a bleak evocation of early-'80s Britain) and *'Start!'*, with its *"What you give is what you get"* manifesto. The Beatles must have liked the latter, by the way: even though the guitar and bass riffs are exact copies of the ones in Taxman, from the Fabs' 1966 album *Revolver*, the Jam were never sued.

Like their contemporaries the Police, also a pop/rock trio led by a singer who later headed off to a much more successful solo band, the Jam had a short-lived but prolific career. Unlike the Police, the Jam have never reformed for a comeback tour, although offers to do so have presumably been coming their way. For the foreseeable future, it appears that fans will have to be satisfied with the songs on this and the other Jam releases.

Track List

SIDE A

Track 1: Pretty Green
Track 2: Monday
Track 3: But I'm Different Now
Track 4: Set The House Ablaze
Track 5: Start!
Track 6: That's Entertainment

SIDE B

Track 1: Dream Time
Track 2: Man In The Corner Shop
Track 3: Music For The Last Couple
Track 4: Boy About Town
Track 5: Scrape Away

The Jam playing in Newcastle upon Tyne during their Trans-Global Unity tour

Nebraska

Bruce Springsteen

Release Date: 1982 | **Record Label:** Columbia Records

Between *The River*, a 1980 double album which was immense in its scope and vision, and 1984's *Born In The USA*, a giant hit, Bruce Springsteen recorded an album that was subtler in all possible ways — 1982's *Nebraska*. Plain in instrumentation and presented with stark artwork, this atypical record may not be Springsteen's loudest, brashest or most vivid work, but it's definitely one of his most emotional.

The creation of the album makes for a fascinating story. Springsteen recorded the whole thing solo, on a four-track tape recorder, in the bedroom of his home in January 1982. Using mostly acoustic guitar, a drum machine and a few extra instruments such as mandolin and organ, he created a suite of dark, folk-influenced songs that took a sombre view of life in America.

The title track was based on the tale of Charles Starkweather, a serial killer from the '50s, while *'Atlantic City'* considered the tale of a man forced to take a job in the criminal underworld. *'Johnny 99'* was about a factory worker who is laid off and kills a man in his desperation, and *'Highway Patrolman'* concerns a police officer who lets his brother escape justice even though he has committed a murder. It's powerful stuff, and a long way from the pyrotechnics of the albums which preceded and followed it.

Once Springsteen had demoed the songs, he attempted to record them with his group, the famous E Street Band, but he was unhappy with the results, feeling that the natural sound of the demos had been lost in translation. In the end the demo tracks were used for the final album, quite a feat as Springsteen had been carrying the cassette around in his pocket for weeks, not even storing it in a case. Noise on the tape had to be filtered out with studio technology, but this was achieved — perhaps miraculously — and the resulting album went on to become something of a gem in Springsteen's catalogue.

Track List

SIDE A
Track 1: Nebraska
Track 2: Atlantic City
Track 3: Mansion On The Hill
Track 4: Johnny 99
Track 5: Highway Patrolman
Track 6: State Trooper
SIDE B
Track 1: Used Cars
Track 2: Open All Night
Track 3: My Father's House
Track 4: Reason To Believe

Springsteen recorded *Nebraska* on his own

The Great Twenty Eight

Chuck Berry

Release Date: 1982 | **Record Label:** Various/Chess

Compilations rarely feature in best album lists, but not every compilation is like *The Great Twenty Eight*. First released in 1982 on Chess Records, it arguably highlights not only the greatest songs of Chuck Berry's illustrious career, but also the ones that helped create the concept of rock and roll. It's an incredibly important album as its carefully picked songs inspired everyone from John Lennon and Ted Nugent, to Bob Dylan and Bruce Springsteen.

The Great Twenty Eight features all the elements that made Berry's song capture the attention of the world's youth when they were first released in the mid'50s and early '60s. 'Maybellene', the compilation's opener starts with a brilliant guitar intro, *'Sweet Little Sixteen's'* distinctive riffs were used wholesale by The Beach Boys who added new lyrics and created *'Surfin USA'*, *'Johnny B. Goode'* features one of the most iconic guitars riffs of all time and formed a centre point of the hit'80s film *Back To The Future*. *'No Particular Place To Go'* features playful lyrics of the kind that could be found throughout Berry's music, while *'Carol'* is such a brilliant piece of work that it's been covered by everyone from The Rolling Stones and The Beatles to Status Quo, The Doors, Tom Petty And The Heartbreakers and even AC/DC. The end result is an epic history that

Chuck Berry in recording studio

fully encapsulates one of music's greatest genres, the fact that it comes from one person's body of work is simply staggering. There's inevitably a few weaker links in an otherwise impressive chain of work, but there's no denying Berry's sheer reach and influence when you listen to this extensive body of work.

Track List

SIDE A
Track 1: Maybellene
Track 2: Thirty Days
Track 3: You Can't Catch Me
Track 4: Too Much Monkey Business
Track 5: Brown Eyed Handsome Man
Track 6: Roll Over Beethoven
Track 7: Havana Moon

SIDE B
Track 1: School Days
Track 2: Rock And Roll Music
Track 3: Oh Baby Doll
Track 4: Reelin' And Rockin'
Track 5: Sweet Little Sixteen
Track 6: Johnny B. Goode
Track 7: Around And Around

SIDE C
Track 1: Seven Nation Army
Track 2: Beautiful Delilah
Track 3: Memphis
Track 4: Sweet Little Rock And Roller
Track 5: Little Queenie
Track 6: Almost Grown
Track 7: Back In The U.S.A.

SIDE D
Track 1: Let It Rock
Track 2: Bye Bye Johnny
Track 3: I'm Talking About You
Track 4: Come On
Track 5: Nadine (Is It You?)
Track 6: No Particular Place To Go
Track 7: I Want To Be Your Driver

Love Over Gold

Dire Straits

Release Date: 1982 | **Record Label:** Warner Bros

The Dire Straits performing live on stage in 1982

You've probably immediately flicked through the contents of this book and wondered where the hell *Brothers In Arms* **is.** While we'd agree that Dire Straits' follow-up album is an excellent piece of work that's worthy of coverage, we'd argue that it's more associated with the rise of the CD and that this gem from 1982 is a far more interesting record, with an equally eye-catching piece of cover art.

Releasing an album that starts with a 14-minute song might sound like commercial suicide, but writer Mark Knopfler had no intention of following cash, he just wanted to craft a collection of epic tunes. As it turned out the cash would follow anyway, with *Love Over Gold* reaching #1 in the UK album charts and staying in the top 100 for a total of 200 weeks (*Brothers In Arms* would eventually top it with 228 weeks).

Recorded at New York's Power Station in just over nine weeks and produced solely by Knopfler, the *Love Over Gold* recording sessions are notable for producing a number of songs that never made it to the final album, including *'The Way It Always Starts'*, *'Badges'*, *'Posters'*, *'Stickers And T-Shirts'* and the excellent *'Private Dancer'*, which ended up on Tina Turner's comeback album. In addition to being a stunning showcase for Knopfler's compositions and delicate guitar work, the recording sessions also allowed for him to use a huge number of his beloved guitars that were in his collection, including an Ovation classic guitar, his 1937 National Steel guitar and his four Schecter Stratocasters.

The huge success of *Love Over Gold* and the sheer accessibility of vinyl during the '80s means it's possible to pick it up for under a fiver. It's a paltry price to pay for such an interesting album and allows you to judge for yourself if opening with the 14-minute *'Telegraph Road'* was such a bad idea (it wasn't).

Track List

SIDE A
Track 1: Telegraph Road
Track 2: Private Investigations
SIDE B
Track 1: Industrial Disease
Track 2: Love Over Gold
Track 3: It Never Rains

Off The Bone

The Cramps

Release Date: 1983 | Record Label: Illegal

One of the first punk rock bands in the mid-'70s emerging with other CBGB bands like the Ramones, the Cramps were also founders of psychobilly, a form a rockabilly that mixed its looks with punk and horror imagery. The band was founded in 1973 by husband and wife group of Lux Interior and Poison Ivy and have gone through countless line-up changes.

As with a lot of the Cramps' albums, *Off The Bone* has a number of rockabilly covers from *'The Way I Walk'* to *'Surfin' Bird'* that the band tweak to make their own. Due to the minimalist drums and lack of bass guitar, the focus lies on the dual guitars and the singing style of Lux Interior who adds a menacing tone with his haunting vocals.

It's hard to know where the cover songs end and the originals begin, as the Cramps were influenced by the '50s sound and their own material sounds like it was taken form that place in time and then fused with their camp humour and B-movie atmosphere.

The record is a UK-only compilation album that collects the entirety of their first EP *Gravest Hits* and includes other songs from their first two studio albums. A year later the album was released in the US as *Bad Music For Bad People*, but it had fewer tracks and seen as a weaker release compared to *Off The Bone*.

The Cramps in 1982

The vinyl release of *Off The Bone* has an Anaglyphic 3D image on the sleeve (the red and cyan picture) with a pair of anaglyphic glasses inside to get the full effect. All of the other versions of the album such as the CD release only have the artwork in plain black and white, loosing some of the quirkiness that the band always put into their work.

Track List

SIDE A
Track 1: Human Fly
Track 2: The Way I Walk
Track 3: Domino
Track 4: Surfin' Bird
Track 5: Lonesome Town
Track 6: Garbageman
Track 7: Fever

SIDE B
Track 1: Drug Train
Track 2: Love Me
Track 3: I Can't Hardly Stand it
Track 4: Goo Goo Muck
Track 5: She Said
Track 6: The Crusher
Track 7: Save it
Track 8: New Kind of Kick

Purple Rain

Prince

Release Date: 1984 | **Record Label:** Warner Bros.

The late Prince was a musical phenomenon, experienced in playing numerous instruments, on his debut album *For You* he played all 27 that were used on the record. *Purple Rain* was the first album to feature Prince's backing group the Revolution. They made the album sound grander, except for *'When Doves Cry'* which noticeably omits the bass guitar.

The album was used as the soundtrack for the film of the same name also staring Prince. That year, the film won the academy award for 'Best Original Song Score,' the last time that the award was given.

With *Purple Rain*, Prince became the first artist to have the number one single, album and film in the US at the same time. The success of both the *Purple Rain* album and film would make Prince one of the biggest male pop stars at the time, second only to the King of Pop, Michael Jackson. The album shows his trademark blend of funk, pop, dance and rock. It's easy to forget that as well as being a great songwriter Prince was also an incredible guitarist and he showcases his skills a couple of times in the album in tracks like the titular *'Purple Rain'*, *'Let's Go Crazy'* and *'When Doves Cry'*.

The record had five top ten singles, but perhaps the song that made the biggest impact on the music industry wasn't even a single, *'Darling Nikki'* led to the introduction of the Parent Advisory stickers on album covers due to the song's lyrics about sex and masturbation. When looking to pick up this vinyl check which version you are getting. There's a regular version of *Purple Rain* as well as a 2015 Paisley Park remaster release that was overseen by Prince. The remastered version can be distinguished by its silver border while the original has a white one. As for which one sounds better, the remaster sounds clearer but it all comes down to preference.

Prince performs live at the Fabulous Forum on 19 February 1985 in Inglewood, California

Track List

SIDE A
Track 1: Let's Go Crazy
Track 2: Take Me With U
Track 3: The Beautiful Ones
Track 4: Comuter Blue
Track 5: Darling Nikki
SIDE B
Track 1: When Doves Cry
Track 2: I Would Die 4 U
Track 3: Baby I'm A Star
Track: 4 Purple Rain

Kate Bush

Hounds Of Love

Hounds Of Love

Kate Bush

Release Date: 1985 | Record Label: EMI

The '80s have been by far the most prolific decade of the British songwriter Kate Bush's career so far: she released four albums in that period, the most experimental of which was *The Dreaming* (1982) and the most commercially successful *Hounds Of Love* ('85). Loaded with hit singles and sharp, precise songs that cut deep to the bone of the human condition, *Hounds* was a reaction to the obscure themes of its predecessor — and widely admired for exactly that reason.

Bush, then as now one of the most accomplished composers and artistic visionaries of her generation, secured our attention this time with the album's first

People fell in love with the amazing music and mysterious vibes

single, *'Running Up That Hill (A Deal With God)'*. With a synth hook that wouldn't go away once you heard it, and a virtuoso vocal performance from Bush which makes today's giant-lunged X-Factor singers seem utterly outclassed, the song remains one of her best known, even more so than the songs from her Wuthering Heights era.

'Cloudbusting', accompanied by a video boasting the best special effects the mid-'80s could muster, continued Bush's presence in the charts and radio, as did *'The Big Sky'* and the title track itself. Note that the singer rarely took the time to explain her lyrical themes with much clarity, leaving it to the listener to decipher what a big sky and so on actually were — but the public didn't mind, lining up to buy Bush's records and tickets for her gigs. There's something very British about that: it wasn't the videos or the words that sold *Hounds Of Love* to us, it was the amazing music and the mysterious vibe of Bush herself.

Although Bush has released albums of similar quality in the three decades since *Hounds Of Love*, none has been quite as commercially successful. She touched a nerve in 1985 that resounded long and loud, leaving us with a suite of songs to which, like all her work, many singer-songwriters since then owe a greater or lesser debt.

Track List

SIDE A

Track 1: Running Up That Hill (A Deal With God)
Track 2: Hounds Of Love
Track 3: The Big Sky
Track 4: Mother Stands For Comfort
Track 5: Cloudbusting

SIDE B

Track 1: And Dream Of Sheep
Track 2: Under Ice
Track 3: Waking The Witch
Track 4: Watching You Without Me
Track 5: Jig Of Life
Track 6: Hello Earth
Track 7: The Morning Fog

Somewhere In Time

Iron Maiden

Release Date: 1986 | **Record Label:** EMI

The veteran British heavy metallers Iron Maiden, now close to 40 years into their career, already felt like seasoned warhorses of heavy metal as far back as 1986, when they released *Somewhere In Time*, the sixth album of their classic initial seven-album run. The reason to acquire this excellent LP on vinyl is simply because of its incredible artwork, which stretches across both front and back and which is a mass of intricate detail. Artist Derek Riggs squeezed in dozens of references to Maiden's previous albums and their personal foibles, from the digital clock reading 23:58 — referring to their song *'2 Minutes To Midnight'* — and the football score readout of West Ham - 7, Arsenal - 3, a nod to bandleader Steve Harris's favourite team.

Smith, Harris, Murray and Gers performing in 2017

Musically, *SIT* is a blend of expert metal noodling from the familiar Maiden school of virtuosity, epic fantasy-fiction themes and yodelling choruses from singer Bruce Dickinson. Primary songwriter Harris didn't compose a concept album as such, despite the many references to time — but he did have a keen eye on the charts, penning enduring singalong hits such as *'Wasted Years'*, *'Heaven Can Wait'* and the title track. Perhaps the most memorable tune is *'Stranger In A Strange Land'*, inspired by the classic Robert Heinlein novel of the same name.

Somewhere In Time represents a jumping-off point for Iron Maiden. After this album, they moved into synthesiser-led, progressive territory, an approach which peaked with their next LP, *Seventh Son Of A Seventh Son*. Within a couple of years of that particular landmark album, Dickinson and Smith jumped ship, heavy metal was subsumed for a decade by grunge and alternative rock, and Maiden entered their own 'wasted years'.

Although Dickinson's replacement Blaze Bayley, of the band Wolfsbane, did his best over a couple of substandard albums, we all breathed a sigh of relief when Dickinson and Smith rejoined at the end of the '90s. Since then, Maiden have ruled the heavy metal roost once again, with Metallica the planet's only bigger metal band.

Dave Murray and Janick Gers

Track List

SIDE A

Track 1: Caught Somewhere In Time
Track 2: Wasted Years
Track 3: Sea Of Madness
Track 4: Heaven Can Wait

SIDE B

Track 1: The Loneliness Of The Long Distance Runner
Track 2: Stranger In A Strange Land
Track 3: Deja-Vu
Track 4: Alexander The Great

The Queen Is Dead

The Smiths

Release Date: 1986 | **Record Label:** Rough Trade

The Smiths were the ultimate Marmite band of British guitar rock. You either admired singer Stephen Morrissey's vocals for their emotive, vibrato-heavy, occasionally slightly flat vigour, or you thought he sounded like a miserable git who couldn't sing. The same went for his lyrics — often sarcastic, morbid and self-pitying — and his image, a bequiffed studenty look with gladioli falling out of his back pocket, plus an NHS hearing aid and glasses.

But you can't fault the music, peaking here on The Smiths' third album of four, thanks to a wide-ranging production from Morrissey and the band's guitarist and songwriter Johnny Marr. In almost all ways the creative powerhouse of the band — while Morrissey added his unique worldview — Marr was the most accomplished guitarist and composer of his genre and demographic. His understanding of how to evoke emotion in music was far-reaching, while his core approach — a rich, chiming guitar sound with arpeggiated chords,

> **"The sheer volume of territory they cover between them is one of the album's most enduring assets"**

often layered for maximum impact — defined the jangly sound of British indie for a decade and more. Bassist Andy Rourke, too, was a master of his instrument, and while drummer Mike Joyce was adequate rather than scintillating at his craft, he and Rourke made up one of the '80s' great rhythm sections.

On *The Queen Is Dead*, all four musicians combined their skills to breathtaking effect. The sheer volume of territory they cover between them is one of the album's most enduring assets, from the big singles on down to the lesser cuts. The record's best-known songs are *'Bigmouth Strikes Again'*, *'The Boy With The Thorn In His Side'* and *'There Is A Light That Never Goes Out'* — all more or less introspective compositions that sealed the Smiths' reputation as songs for sad people.

This over-simple analysis does the songs and the band a disservice, though. 'Bigmouth...' begins with a sweet acoustic intro and a restless bass-line that owes a debt to classic funk: in fact, it's musically hyperactive throughout, with only

Track List

SIDE A
- **Track 1:** The Queen Is Dead
- **Track 2:** Frankly, Mr Shankly
- **Track 3:** I Know It's Over
- **Track 4:** Never Had No One Ever
- **Track 5:** Cemetry Gates

SIDE B
- **Track 1:** Bigmouth Strikes Again
- **Track 2:** The Boy With The Thorn In His Side
- **Track 3:** Vicar In A Tutu
- **Track 4:** There Is A Light That Never Goes Out
- **Track 5:** Some Girls Are Bigger Than Ours

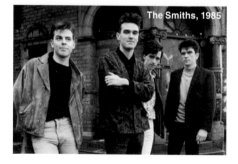

The Smiths, 1985

People either loved
Morrissey or hated him

Morrissey's sideways lyric about Joan of Arc burning at the stake (*"as her Walkman started to melt"*). Artificially falsettoed vocals, wailing guitar lines in the background, punchy licks picked at great speed: all of studio life was here.

As for *'The Boy With The Thorn In His Side'* and *'There Is A Light That Never Goes Out'*, these did deserve their reputation as bedroom anthems for sociopathic teenagers to an extent. The former was musically joyous, while its lyrics appeared to be sung from the perspective of a kid suffering from crippling shyness. *'There Is A Light…'* encapsulates the fears of the '80s teenager with perfect naivety: it's impossible to hear the lines *"Oh, please don't drop me home, because I haven't got one"* and *"If a double-decker bus crashes into us / To die by your side / What a heavenly way to die"* without instantly visualising the mockery of all the Smiths-haters in the world. Morrissey meant those words, though, and sang them unashamedly.

The Queen Is Dead wasn't all introspection, of course. Morrissey was, above all, an educated writer with an urge to communicate his vocabulary — and invoking Keats and Yeats on Cemetry Gates and 'loud loutish lovers' on *'I Know It's Over'*, he did just that. You might not have enjoyed his evident desire to provoke, or how deeply he plumbed the depths of psychic misery in his lyrics, but one thing was for sure, he never bored you.

There's outright fun to be had here, too. Go to *'Vicar In A Tutu'* for the sound of a band delivering a tongue-in-cheek rockabilly sound with perfect accuracy. Then there's the crystal clarity and icy tones of the guitars in *'Some Girls Are Bigger Than Others'*, a lyrically flippant but musically divine song that leads you to wonder what the hell they were actually on about, on this and the other three Smiths albums. We still don't really know the answer, all these years later, and the Smiths' catalogue is all the richer for it.

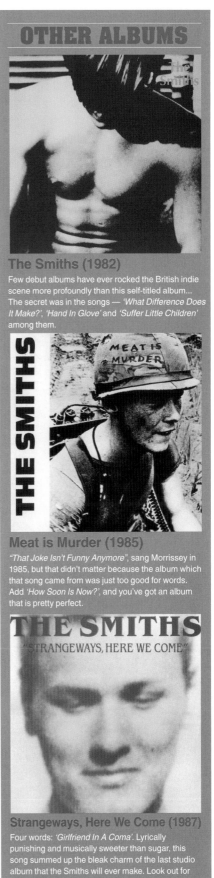

OTHER ALBUMS

The Smiths (1982)

Few debut albums have ever rocked the British indie scene more profoundly than this self-titled album... The secret was in the songs — *'What Difference Does It Make?'*, *'Hand In Glove'* and *'Suffer Little Children'* among them.

Meat is Murder (1985)

"That Joke Isn't Funny Anymore", sang Morrissey in 1985, but that didn't matter because the album which that song came from was just too good for words. Add *'How Soon Is Now?'*, and you've got an album that is pretty perfect.

Strangeways, Here We Come (1987)

Four words: *'Girlfriend In A Coma'*. Lyrically punishing and musically sweeter than sugar, this song summed up the bleak charm of the last studio album that the Smiths will ever make. Look out for endless reissues and repackages.

Raising Hell

Run-DMC

Release Date: 1986 | **Record Label:** Profile Records

Run-DMC certainly didn't conceive hip hop. In fact The Sugarhill Gang's Rapper's Delight — widely regarded as the first successful single of the genre — had been released six years prior to Run-DMC's third album, *Raising Hell*.

However the 12-track LP kickstarted a golden age of hip hop, dismissing the notion that the genre was a fad as it grabbed a top 10 spot in the US charts. *Raising Hell* remains the trio's most successful album, selling over a million copies in its first month and going on to achieve triple platinum status.

It's impossible to discuss the album without giving a nod to the groundbreaking collaboration with Aerosmith on *'Walk This Way'*. It wasn't the first time Run-DMC had experimented with a fusion of rock and hip hop, having done so on earlier tracks Rock Box and King of Rock. Producer Rick Rubin suggested the cover during recording sessions for the album, met at first with trepidation from Run and DMC who had no idea who Aerosmith were at the time. The pioneering collaboration catapulted Run-DMC to stardom, as well as leading to a revival for Aerosmith. Achieving substantial worldwide success, *'Walk This Way'* did more to popularise hip hop to the masses than any other previous song.

Raising Hell offers more than just the one iconic track. Lead single *'My Adidas'*, the hilarious *'You Be Illin'* and sample-driven classic *'It's Tricky'* are all further proof of the energy and charisma propping up Run-DMC's unique sound. Often favouring the superficial over subtext over the course of the album, *Raising Hell* conversely concludes with *'Proud To Be Black''s* rant on society's racial tensions.

Featuring a photograph of Run and DMC, the record's jacket was available in two distinct colour schemes — either purple with red reverse or a green cover with blue reverse. Both versions of the LP have identical track listings, though some early copies mislabelled both sides as Side B.

Track List

SIDE A
Track 1: Peter Piper
Track 2: It's Tricky
Track 3: My Adidas
Track 4: Walk This Way
Track 5: Is It Live
Track 6: Perfection
SIDE B
Track 1: Hit It Run
Track 2: Raising Hell
Track 3: You Be Illin'
Track 4: Dumb Girl
Track 5: Son Of Byford
Track 6: Proud To Be Black

Run DMC, New York 1986

Hysteria

Def Leppard

Release Date: 1987 | Record Label: Mercury Records

I f 1983's *Pyromania* had Def Leppard dipping their toe into pop's waters, *Hysteria* was a cannonball at the deep end. From the beginning, the album's concept had remained the same — to be a hard rock version of Michael Jackson's *Thriller*, on which every track could be a hit single (and indeed seven of the 12 tracks were, one more single than *Thriller*). At just over 25 million copies sold worldwide, *Hysteria* remains the band's best-selling record.

Def Leppard's turbocharged fourth record infamously took almost four years to produce and at a cost just shy of $5 million. The band initially wrote songs for *Hysteria* (then called *Animal Instinct*) with Mutt Lange, who had produced their previous two LPs.

Lange quickly dropped out due to a full schedule and was replaced by Jim Steinman, best known for working with Meat Loaf on *Bat Out Of Hell*. But ultimately after creative differences with Steinman and a short hiatus after drummer Rick Allen lost his left arm in a car accident, Lange returned for *Hysteria's* final recording sessions. Def Leppard apologised for the delay in LP's liner notes, also compounded by Lange's own car accident and frontman Joe Elliot's bout of the mumps,

Renowned designer Andie Airfix was responsible for *Hysteria's* artwork, known for his work with Led Zeppelin, Judas Priest and Metallica. Initially working to the title of *Animal Instinct*, he created a cover featuring an eagle, a shark and a lion blending into each other before reworking it into the distorted face of the final release.

At a run time of around 63 minutes, *Hysteria* really stretched the limits of how long a standard album at the time could be — unfortunately for audiophiles, to the detriment of the vinyl pressings. Over an hour's worth of music is way too much to squeeze onto a single platter and retain a high standard of audio quality. More recent vinyl releases of the album remedy this by running over two LPs, most notably the 30th Anniversary gatefold vinyl re-issue, featuring fully remastered tracks on a strikingly translucent orange 180g wax.

Track List

SIDE A
Track 1:	Women
Track 2:	Rocket
Track 3:	Animal
Track 4:	Love Bites
Track 5:	Pour Some Sugar On Me
Track 6:	Armageddon It

SIDE B
Track 1:	Gods Of War
Track 2:	Don't Shoot Shotgun
Track 3:	Run Riot
Track 4:	Hysteria
Track 5:	Excitable
Track 6:	Love And Affection

Joe Elliott lead singer of Def Leppard

Mick Hutson/Redferns

Bad

Michael Jackson

Release Date: 1987 | Record Label: Epic/CBS

Five years had passed since the release of *Thriller*, the album that had become the best selling record in the world, so naturally there were great expectations for the follow-up. In the years after *Thriller's* release Michael Jackson had begun to make a reputation for himself in the newspapers, he reportedly had a number of different plastic surgery operations to change his face, he was sleeping in a hyperbaric chamber to slow down the ageing process and he had a chimpanzee called Bubbles who would go with Jackson on his tours. This led fans and the public to wonder if Jackson was going to loose his touch when it came to making his music, but there was no doubt that *Bad* would sell in the millions regardless. There were reportedly eight times the normal advance orders of a major LP release for *Bad* compared to other albums of the time.

To add to the public's worry of the album's quality, radio stations were not allowed to play any if it on air before it's release. It wasn't until the record went on sale that radio stations were allowed to play it, which

at the time seemed counterproductive. Normally a record would receive a week of air-time before its initial release. Whether the record label didn't want people recording the songs onto tape, or they just didn't want the public to hear it without buying it first is still unknown, but the album was still a massive hit upon it's release. In the United States, *Bad* was given a lot of publicity. American Broadcaster CBS aired a TV special on Jackson's life and career, titled *Michael Jackson: The Magic Returns*. At the end of the documentary, they debuted the video for the titular track *'Bad'*, the 18-minute-long short film directed by Martin Scorsese. While *Bad* didn't go on to beat *Thriller*, it would set its own record for sales in terms of its singles. It became the first album in history to have five of its singles peak at #1 consecutively on the Billboard Hot 100. This record is yet to be beaten, although Katy Perry came close in 2011.

Jackson reportedly wrote 60 songs for *Bad*, 30 of them were recorded as he was hoping to release *Bad* as a three-disc album. He was eventually talked into releasing it as a ten track LP, with eight

> **"It became the first album to have five singles peak at #1 consecutively"**

Track List

SIDE A
Track 1: Bad
Track 2: The Way You Make Me Feel
Track 3: Speed Demon
Track 4: Liberian Girl
Track 5: Just Good Friends
SIDE B
Track 1: Another Part Of Me
Track 2: Man In The Mirror
Track 3: I Just Can't Stop Loving You
Track 4: Dirty Diana
Track 5: Smooth Criminal

Jackson was the most successful pop star of the '80s

of the tracks being composed by Jackson himself. The album takes a more serious and adult tone in it's songs, with less disco-inspired tracks and more darker or moodier tracks such as *'Dirty Diana'* and *'Liberian Girl'*. The vocal eccentricities like the 'shamone', hiccups and high-pitched 'hee hees' that everyone has come to expect of Michael Jackson all came to prominence in this album. All but two tracks on the album were released as singles, *'Speed Demon'* was only released as a promotional single for the radio and *'Just Good Friends'* was never actually released as a single in any form.

Bad saw Jackson reach new heights in the music industry once again. It was the first album to top the charts in 25 countries and was the best-selling album worldwide between 1987 and 1988. The *Bad* tour broke a Guinness World Record when 504,000 people attended seven sold-out Wembley Arena shows.

It was also in 1988 *Michael Jackson's Moonwalker* was released. The direct-to-video movie featured a series of short films which were long music videos for songs from the *Bad* album and staring Jackson himself. It topped the music video charts for 22 weeks until another Michael Jackson video *Michael Jackson: The Legend Continues* took its place. With the success of *Bad*, *Moonwalker* and his autobiography all in the space of a few years, Jackson was the most successful pop star of the '80s, which rightfully earned him the title King of Pop.

OTHER ALBUMS

Thriller (1982)
The best selling of all time and for good reason. Sticking with the mix of pop, R&B and disco and adding new genres such as hard rock with *'Beat It'* that featured one of the greatest guitar solos of all time from Van Halen.

Dangerous (1991)
The extravagant cover is worth the purchase alone. Jackson would again write the majority of the songs but the subjects he wrote about would be more varied, focusing on problems in the world he wanted to help change.

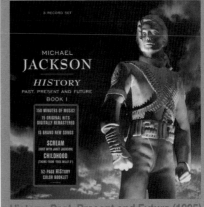

History: Past, Present and Future (1995)
30 tracks over three LPs, the first three sides feature his a compilation of his greatest hits while the second is entirely new material feature some of Michael Jackson's most personal lyrics on topics such as suicide and paranoia.

After the success of Thriller it wasn't known if *Bad* would do as well

Appetite For Destruction

Guns N' Roses

Release Date: 1987 | Record Label: Geffen

After the original line up split Guns N' Roses lost a lot of their lustre, it's easy to forget just how big the band's debut album was. To this day *Appetite For Destruction* is the best selling debut album to this day and is one of the best selling albums of all time. Guns N' Roses brought an edge to rock music inside and outside the studio that hadn't been seen since the Rolling Stones days. *Appetite For Destruction* features the singles *'Welcome To The Jungle'*, *'Sweet Child O' Mine'* and *'Paradise City'*, which all made it to the top ten in the US charts. The opening of *'Welcome To The Jungle'* perfectly captures you

by teasing with light echoing guitar before building and then exploding into the blues-grooving main riff. Some songs featured in Guns N' Roses' later albums such as *'November Rain'* and *'You Could Be Mine'* were written, and originally intended, to be recorded for *Appetite* but these were not used for different reasons. Rather then having a Side A and Side B, *Appetite For Destruction* has a G and R Side, with the Guns side featuring the songs on drugs and life in Hollywood and the Roses side comprised of songs on love and sex.

The original vinyl release had a different cover to the iconic Celtic cross with the skull of each band

member. The first release of the record featured artwork by Robert Williams of a woman being sexually assaulted by a robot and a monster about to attack the robot. Stores refused to stock the album and the record label replaced the artwork with the one we all know.

The version with the banned artwork isn't hard to find if you look through online auction sites, but you should expect to pay at least double what you would for the same album with the reissued artwork.

Track List

SIDE A
Track 1: Welcome To The Jungle
Track 2: It's So Easy
Track 3: Nightrain
Track 4: Out Ta Get Me
Track 5: Mr. Brownstone
Track 6: Paradise City
SIDE B
Track 1: My Michelle
Track 2: Think About You
Track 3: Sweet Child O' Mine
Track 4: You're Crazy
Track 5: Anything Goes
Track 6: Rocket Queen

Guns N' Roses perform in concert at the Ritz on 2 February 1988 in New York City

Dèche à la Ch'touille

Tulaviok

Release Date: 1987 | **Record Label:** Dirty Punk Records

Formed in 1984, the French punk band Tulaviok were only around for a very short five years, but over the time that they shared together, they earned a reputation for their eccentric nature, merchandise and even the design of their record, CD and LP sleeves. On their tours they would sell underwear with silly images on them, but their most infamous piece was the 1987 vinyl (and album in question) *Dèche à la Ch'touille*. The band were no strangers to phallic humour, with their mascot being a penis, their own record label called Bollocks Produktion, and the title of this very album roughly translated to mean 'dick with gonorrhoea' (with a penis motif also included, if you didn't think there were quite enough penis' already). The run of this unique vinyl was limited to only 5,000 copies, which is enough to make most vinyl collectors want it. What really makes it an album worth owning in pressed form is the 15" pop-out erect penis, making it an album that really is like no other out there — even to this day. The tracklist can be found

on the testicles of this pop-out, and the rest of the vinyl gatefold is filled photographs making up a collage of random photos taken by the band, some that are certainly more NSFW than others…

Due to its cult status, the vinyl is highly sought after by collectors and it rarely comes on online auction sites. But on the rare occasion that one has surfaced on the pages of the web, the album typically goes for between £60-85. *Dèche à la Ch'touille* was rereleased on CD in 2009 and the infamous pop-up penis were replaced with a foldout book, penis included. However, this is also very hard to find but isn't as sought after or rare as the original vinyl release. As for the album itself, it's a loud, typically fast and gritty hard-core punk album that was popularised in the late '70s/early '80s with the help of bands like Dead Kennedys and Black Flag. The track list is made up of 13 'banter songs', which violated

taboos and were arguably the band's speciality. The LP's sleeve looks like someone has scribbled all of the songs' lyrics on it, along with some doodles including yes, you guessed right, even more penises.

> **"What really makes it an album worth owning on vinyl is the 15" pop-out erect penis, making it an album that really is like no other out there"**

Track List

SIDE A
Track 1: Les Filles De Camaret
Track 2: Cathy
Track 3: Caroline La Postipute
Track 4: Adieu Fais-Toi Putain
Track 5: Nina Ma Poupée
Track 6: Gros Dégueulasse
Track 7: Vive La Merde
SIDE B
Track 1: Zob—Zob-Zob
Track 2: Pére Du Panloup
Track 3: Sac A Gnôle
Track 4: De Profondis
Track 5: Faits Comme Des Rats
Track 6: Tulaviok

Surfer Rosa

Pixies

Release Date: 1988 | Record Label: 4AD

The Boston band Pixies (note: not 'The' Pixies, there is no article here) were responsible for a lot, not least the sound of more or less scratchy, jangly indie band you listened to in the '90s. Nirvana in particular owed the group a serious debt, as their singer Kurt Cobain stated: he even used Pixies producer Steve Albini for his own third album.

The secret behind Pixies' music, at least on their *Surfer Rosa*, the 1988 debut album we're discussing here, was that the songs' abrasive textures rested on real pop melodies that you could hum in the bath while still rocking out. The guitars were often heavyweight and the bass prominent, but the songs — whether sung by guitarist Frank 'Black Francis' Black or bassist Kim Deal — were still catchy as hell. The overall vibe was anarchic and a little chaotic, with Albini's sympathetic production making you feel as though you were in the group's rehearsal room with them. For example, you can hear the untrained singers actually gasping for breath during the song *'River Euphrates'*: that's how real this album was.

This all allowed the songs to ring through with real emotion. *'Gigantic'*, the cut for which Deal — and possibly the band in general — is best known, is at heart a sweet love song, while *'Where Is My Mind?'* lies somewhere between an acoustic whimsy

(Radiohead's *'Nice Dream'* comes to mind) and an arena anthem made up of layers of drone guitar. Then there's *'Break My Body'*, a classic album-opener of its era: in this single song, much of the band's ethos appears, from guitar tracks that don't quite match up — and are proud of it — to a super-live drum and bass sound. It's all here.

Throughout the iconic LP, the band don't neglect their songwriting dynamics, building the songs and allowing them to fall again. In doing so, Pixies amassed a fanbase that is enduring to this day, even though the group currently tours and records with a revised line-up (Deal left the band in 2013, replaced briefly by Kim Shattuck in 2013 and then with Paz Lenchantin from 2014). Few bands can match their legacy.

Track List

SIDE A
Track 1: Bone Machine
Track 2: Break My Body
Track 3: Something Against You
Track 4: Broken Face
Track 5: Gigantic
Track 6: River Euphrates
SIDE B
Track 1: Where Is My Mind?
Track 2: Cactus
Track 3: Tony's Theme
Track 4: Oh My Golly!
Track 5: Vamos
Track 6: I'm Amazed
Track 7: Brick Is Red

The Pixies in 2016

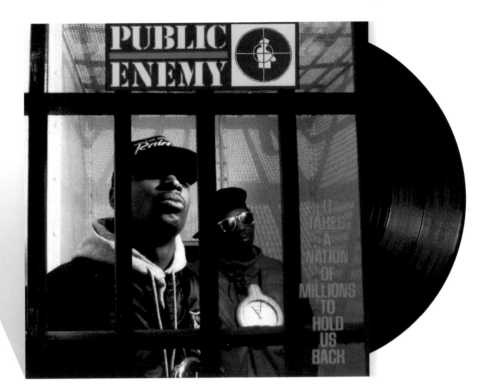

It Takes A Nation Of Millions To Hold Us Back

Public Enemy

Release Date: 1998 | **Record Label:** Def Jam

Before 1988 the best hip-hop was powerful, convincing protest music: the difficulty was getting it to a widespread audience, saturated as fans were by lightweight 'party' hip-hop that meant practically nothing. After Public Enemy's second album *It Takes A Nation Of Millions To Hold Us Back*, that all changed: along with Ice-T and NWA, PE made the music a vehicle for their expressions of black awareness — and appropriately, nations of millions were listening.

The rhymes delivered by bandleader Carlton 'Chuck D' Ridenour atop the layered mountains of samples collated by Hank Shocklee and his Bomb Squad production team were uncompromising, while

Flavor Flav, 1991

Chuck's fellow rappers William 'Flavor Flav' Drayton and Norman 'Terminator X' Rogers added their own vitriolic barbs to the mix. The big songs — *'Bring The Noise'*, *'Don't Believe The Hype'* and *'She Watch Channel Zero?!'* — have lost not an iota of their power over the ensuing years.

Politically, this album stood alone. Sure, the aforementioned Ice-T and NWA were making serious music by '88, but the former focused on lamenting the violence of gang culture, while the latter glorified it. All three acts served to raise awareness of the plight of the young black male at the hands of racist organisations, but only Public Enemy offered any form of positive solution.

In some ways, *It Takes A Nation Of Millions...* could never be recorded these days. As the music industry has come to recognise the value of sampling — thanks to new, innovative music being thinner on the ground than it used to be, perhaps — the costs of using the samples found on this record would render it too expensive to create. Any modern hip-hop producer would baulk at the idea of using the introduction of Queen's iconic *'Flash's Theme'*, as the Bomb Squad do on *'Terminator X To The Edge Of Panic'*.

We're lucky that albums of this magnitude were created before the opportunity to do so faded away.

Track List

SIDE A
Track 1: Countdown To Armageddon
Track 2: Bring The Noise
Track 3: Don't Believe The Hype
Track 4: Cold Lampin' With Flavor
Track 5: Terminator X To The Edge Of Panic
Track 6: Mind Terrorist
Track 7: Louder Than A Bomb
Track 8: Caught, Can We Get A Witness?

SIDE B
Track 1: Show 'Em Whatcha Got
Track 2: She Watch Channel Zero?!
Track 3: Night Of The Living Baseheads
Track 4: Black Steel In The Hour Of Chaos
Track 5: Security Of The First World
Track 6: Rebel Without A Pause
Track 7: Prophets Of Rage
Track 8: Party For Your Right To Fight

Paul's Boutique

Beastie Boys

Release Date: 1989 | **Record Label:** Capitol

In theory, the Beastie Boys' second album shouldn't have been a hit — and in fact it both wasn't and was, at the same time. Confused? You will be.

Adam 'MCA' Yauch, Michael 'Mike D' Diamond and Adam 'Ad-Rock' Horowitz had struck gold in 1986 with their debut album, *Licensed To Ill*. The first hip-hop album to come from a white group and make a major impact, *LTI* was a wholly juvenile and entirely appealing set of tunes. You only have to cast your mind back to the singles *'Fight For Your Right'* and *'No Sleep Till Brooklyn'*, with their simple riffs and shouty rhymes about sex and being drunk, for an idea of the album's sophistication level. Despite its raw nature, the album has sold 10 million units and counting, making it a Diamond record.

By rights, its follow-up should have been massive — right? Well, no. At least some of the success of *Licensed To Ill* can be attributed to the presence of Rick Rubin, who produced the album, and who had signed the Beastie Boys to his Def Jam label shortly after they switched from

> **"As the years passed, the music of the Beastie Boys matured and became a serious artform"**

hardcore punk to hip-hop in the mid-'80s. For Paul's Boutique, the band switched from Def Jam to the major label Capitol, severing the Rubin connection and the creative gold which that had brought to the group. Now steering their ship alone, the trio — still only in their early to mid-twenties at the time — sought assistance from the production duo the Dust Brothers (Mike Simpson and John King) for the new album. Seeking a deeper, more layered palette of sounds this time, the band took advantage of a set of instrumental tunes which the producers had recorded previously, intending to release them to clubs. Adding their rhymes and turning the tracks into full songs, the Beastie Boys came up with a vast album of musically complex songs with lyrics that were slightly (operative word: 'slightly') more adult than those on *Licensed To Ill*.

The public's reaction was muted in comparison to the ecstatic response that had greeted the debut album. The Beastie Boys' fanbase had evidently been expecting jagged guitar riffs and songs about frat parties, not the extended funk jams that

Track List

SIDE A
Track 1: To All The Girls
Track 2: Shake Your Rump
Track 3: Johnny Ryall
Track 4: Egg Man
Track 5: High Plains Drifter
Track 6: The Sounds Of Science
Track 7: 3-Minute Rule
Track 8: Hey Ladies
SIDE B
Track 1: 5-Piece Chicken Dinner
Track 2: Looking Down The Barrel Of A Gun
Track 3: Car Thief
Track 4: What Comes Around
Track 5: Shadrach
Track 6: Ask For Janice
Track 7: B-Boy Bouillabaisse
  • 59 Chrystie Street
  • Get On The Mic
  • Stop That Train
  • A Year And A Day
  • Hello Brooklyn
  • Dropping Names
  • Lay It On Me
  • Mike On The Mic
  • A.W.O.L.
Track 8: 33% God (Japan only)
Track 9: Diss Yourself In '89 (Just Do It) (Japan only)

This second album houldn't have been a hit, but it was

populated *Paul's Boutique* — but here's the thing. As the years passed and the music of the Beastie Boys, as well as the entire hip-hop movement, matured and became a serious art form, more and more namechecks began to appear from various places for the record. Chuck D of Public Enemy admitted years later that Paul's Boutique was the 'dirty secret' of the hip-hop community, who admitted privately that better beats were impossible to find.

Seen in that light, a run-through of the songs on the album begins to reveal a ton of hidden treasures. *'The Sounds Of Science'* is a great starting point, not least because the band and producers elected to sample the Beatles on the song: nowadays, such a thing would be impossible, or at the very least punitively expensive — but *Paul's Boutique* was recorded before modern sampling laws had been made, let alone tested in court, and the Beastie Boys got clean away with it. Then there's funk-fests such as *'Hey Ladies'*, loaded with no fewer than 16 classic rock and soul samples, and *'Looking Down The Barrel Of A Gun'*, based on a heavy rock riff from Mountain's *'Mississippi Queen'*.

The album ends with a nine-part suite of rhymes called *'B-Boy Bouillabaisse'*, revealing the depth of songwriting ability which the band had begun to explore, as well as their progressive approach towards album structure. In 1989 hip-hop had not yet reached this level of sophistication, generally speaking, although Public Enemy and NWA were beginning to explore the art of crafting deep music through samples. It's truly remarkable that the move in that direction, which typifies hip-hop to this day, came from three white geeks from Brooklyn obsessed with girls and booze. All these years later, our respect is due.

Were the Beastie Boys a dirty secret of the hip-hop community?

OTHER ALBUMS

Licensed To Ill (1986)

Listening to the sophisticated music that the Beastie Boys made in their later career, it's hard to believe that they started out with an album as reductively simple as *Licensed To Ill*. Snotty to the max, it's best treated as a party record.

Ill Communication (1994)

Discovering irony and becoming one of the first '90s bands to commemorate cheesy '70s culture, with *Ill Communication* the Beastie Boys made a truly funky album to treasure third time out. *'Sabotage'* was one of their coolest ever singles.

Hello Nasty (1998)

After a decade and more in business, the Beastie Boys finally arrived at a sort of maturity with *Hello Nasty*, titled after the phone greeting used by the receptionist at their PR firm Nasty Little Man. *Intergalactic* was the superb lead-off single.

3 Feet High And Rising

De La Soul

Release Date: 1989 | **Record Label:** Tommy Boy/Warner Bros

In a time when gangsta rap was on the rise, most MCs were using rap to boast or describe bleak situations they grew up in and around, De La Soul went a different direction with playful and fun tunes including anti-drug songs. It also helps that the three members of De La Soul were more than capable at spitting rhymes.

The whole of *3 Feet High And Rising* was recorded for $13,000 using only a Casio drum machine/sampler and a harmoniser. Like most hip hop/rap artists, De La Soul used plenty of samples, but the trio would take them from genres that other rappers of the time wouldn't dare touch. Sampling artists such as the Monkees, Hall & Oats and Led Zeppelin to name just a few. The album opens with a skit of the members of De La Soul on a gameshow, while these are almost commonplace now at the beginning of albums or as interludes between tracks, *3 Feet High And Rising* is credited with popularising the concept. It's a quirky album with surreal comedy, but that's what you get when one of the member's name is his favourite food spelled backwards.

Like the topics the group rap about, De La Soul's artwork wasn't like a typical rap cover of its time. While the majority of popular '80s' rap artists, such

De La Soul, Holland, 1989

as Public Enemy and N.W.A, had dark, gritty covers while De La Soul was bright. The inner sleeve of the vinyl had a comic strip printed onto it featuring the group travelling from Mars and talking with a cartoon duck. The members of the group are placed in a circle and the text on the cover is also circular, this is so it needs to be rotated to be read, like how a record needs to be spun to be heard.

Track List

SIDE A
Track 1: Intro
Track 2: The Magic Number
Track 3: Change In Speak
Track 4: Cool Breeze On The Rocks
Track 5: Can U Keep A Secret
Track 6: Jenifa Taught Me (Derwin's Revenge)
Track 7: Ghetto Thang

SIDE B
Track 1: Transmitting Live From Mars
Track 2: Eye Know
Track 3: Take It Off
Track 4: A Little Bit Of Soap
Track 5: Tread Water
Track 6: Potholes In My Lawn

SIDE C
Track 1: Say No Go
Track 2: Do As De La Does
Track 3: Plug Tunin' (Last Chance To Comprehead)
Track 4: De La Orgee
Track 5: Buddy

SIDE C
Track 1: Description
Track 2: Me Myself And I
Track 3: This Is A Recording 4 Living In A Full Time Era (L.I.F.E.)
Track 4: I Can Do Anything (Delacratic)
Track 5: D.A.I.S.Y. Age

The Stone Roses

The Stone Roses

Release Date: 1989 | **Record Label:** Silvertone

The Stone Roses' album was the seed from which Britpop would grow, before Oasis and Blur there were four guys from Manchester who would host their own gigs and not promote them but just let the fans find them. Before Britpop there was the baggy scene. The Stone Roses led the Madchester scene, thanks to the attention brought to them by the magazines *Melody Maker* and NME who covered the scene intensely.

Though the band formed in 1983, their debut album came six years later. In that time they had released singles and switched genre a couple of times, the single *'So Young'* features a fast, more punk-driven sound; *'Sally Cinnamon'* was lighter in tone, almost pop-rock.

Eventually the band would stick with the sounds that defined them and the whole Madchester scene.

The Stone Roses blended dance-influenced drum beats with psychedelic pop guitar tones to create an album that some would describe as '60s-inspired but singer Ian Brown will be the first person to shoot down that assumption.

They would sell out shows in Manchester and around the Northwest but failed to make a broader impact. After their debut album was released the singles got airtime on BBC Radio 1 and they started to sell out across the country. The self-titled record technically wasn't their first album. Not in a rush to put out an album, the band created a record which would later be released as *'Garage Flower'* but at the time they were not please with how it came out, so it wasn't released after it was originally completed. The Stone Roses' album cover was designed by the band's guitarist, John Squire, who took inspiration from Jackson Pollock and the 1968 Paris riots. Squire spoke to a Frenchman who said they would carry lemons with them as they were an antidote to the tear gas that police would use.

Track List

SIDE A
Track 1: I Wanna Be Adored
Track 2: She Bangs The Drums
SIDE B
Track 1: Waterfall
Track 2: Don't Stop
Track 3: Bye Bye Badman
SIDE C
Track 1: Elizabeth My Dear
Track 2: (Song For My) Sugar Spun Sister
Track 3: Made Of Stone
Track 4: Shoot You Down
SIDE D
Track 1: This Is The One
Track 2: I Am The Resurrection

The Stone Roses (Ian Brown, John Squire, Mani and Reni) Manchester, 1989

massiv attack

rage against the

oasis *Definitely Maybe*

SOUNDGARDEN

G O

NIИ

a tribe called Quest

midnight Marauders

OK COMPUTER
RADIOHEAD

'90S

Ten

Pearl Jam

Release Date: 1991 | Record Label: Epic

Ten, while highly regarded as one of the most influential albums of the '90s now, was a slow burner for audiences. It didn't reach the top ten of the Billboard charts until a year after it was released, but it became one of the key albums in the Seattle grunge scene. Although bands like Soundgarden and Alice In Chains had achieved some success, it was Pearl Jam's *Ten* that cemented the genre in the mainstream. Released around the same time as Nirvana's *Nevermind*, grunge fans in 1991 were torn between the punk-infused harshness of Nirvana or the stadium-rock anthem sound that Pearl Jam mixed into *Ten*. Eddie Vedder's vocal style would be emulated by many of the singers who followed in the mid to late '90s, for better or worse. His yells were passionate and deep while the lyrics were introspective, focusing mainly on isolation, but his vocals offered a glimmer of hope.

Just one year prior to recording *Ten*, guitarist Stone Gossard and bassist Jeff Ament decided to part ways after their previous band, Mother Love

Bone, disbanded. They reunited when Gossard had written some new tracks with a different sound. They hired Eddie Vedder after he heard the demo and auditioned, then Pearl Jam went into a studio to record the album three months after the band had officially formed, writing new tracks during the studio time. The sound Gossard had written fused classic rock with some funk-inspired and reverb-fuelled riffs with sweeping choruses that Vedder could accompany with memorable lyrics. There were also the darker, angsty slow songs associated with grunge, such as *'Jeremy'*, written about a high-school student who shot himself in front of his class.

During the recording of the album, the band was known as Mookie Blaylock, after the professional basketball player. It changed its name after signing to Epic Records, but kept the nod to Blaylock by naming the album after the player's jersey number. As for the name Pearl Jam, there are multiple stories as to how the band members chose it, but which one is true is up for debate. Ten remains Pearl Jam's most successful album despite being slow to sell. It was thanks to

> **"Ten remains Pearl Jam's most successful album... in the charts for more than 260 weeks"**

Track List

SIDE A
Track 1: Once
Track 2: Even Flow
Track 3: Alive
Track 4: Why Go
Track 5: Black
Track 6: Jeremy

SIDE B
Track 1: Oceans
Track 2: Porch
Track 3: Garden
Track 4: Deep
Track 5: Release
Track 6: Master/Slave

The rock band from Seattle

the success of the singles *'Even Flow'*, *'Alive'* and especially *'Jeremy'* that pushed *Ten* to eventually sell well, staying in the Billboard charts for more than 260 weeks.

Pearl Jam was never really happy with how the album came out, and would be vocal about how they didn't like the final mix, and eventually the album was remastered in 2009. The remastered edition comes with both versions of *Ten*: the original mix and Brendan O'Brien's remix. Those who grew up loving the sound of the album may be taken back because much of the reverb was removed to give

a clearer overall sound, like an album made in the '00s, but this version feels emptier. The 2009 rerelease is the most common version of the album on vinyl, but you get both versions of the album, so you can listen to both and decide which one you prefer. You could search the web for an original pressing of *Ten* but you would be spending around the same amount of money as you would for a new copy. The rerelease can be distinguished by its white/cream cover with the band in black and white, and much like the sound of the album, it is closer to how the band originally wanted it to turn out.

Pearl Jam refused to adhere to traditional music industry practices, refusing to make proper music videos or give interviews

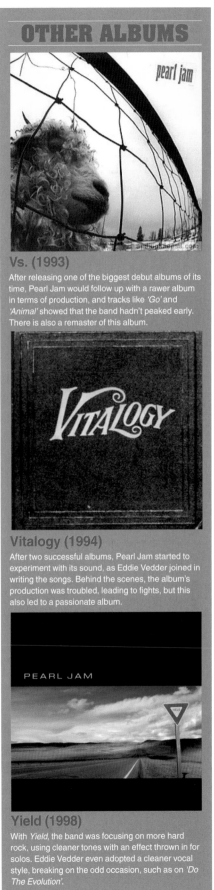

OTHER ALBUMS

Vs. (1993)
After releasing one of the biggest debut albums of its time, Pearl Jam would follow up with a rawer album in terms of production, and tracks like *'Go'* and *'Animal'* showed that the band hadn't peaked early. There is also a remaster of this album.

Vitalogy (1994)
After two successful albums, Pearl Jam started to experiment with its sound, as Eddie Vedder joined in writing the songs. Behind the scenes, the album's production was troubled, leading to fights, but this also led to a passionate album.

Yield (1998)
With *Yield*, the band was focusing on more hard rock, using cleaner tones with an effect thrown in for solos. Eddie Vedder even adopted a cleaner vocal style, breaking on the odd occasion, such as on *'Do The Evolution'*.

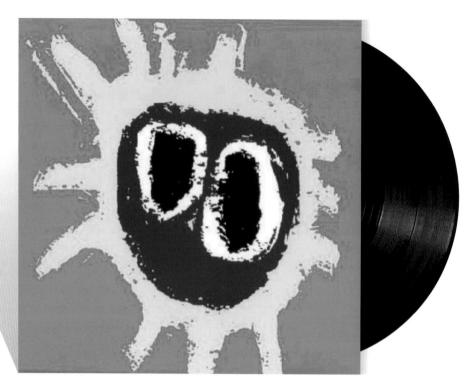

Screamadelica

Primal Scream

Release Date: 1991 | Record Label: Creation

I t's somewhat amazing to think that *Screamadelica's* iconic album image very nearly didn't happen at all. With the album due to launch in the September of 1991, the band was still without a cover just two months before this date in July, and its band mates were desperate to use something that would make as much of a statement as the new direction its music was heading in. In an interview with *Daily Record*, Alan McGee, who was Creation's boss at the time, mentioned that he rejected Bobby Gillespie's original request to feature the band alongside an attractive model, and suggested that they went with the sunburst that had featured on the album's first single, *'Higher Than The Sun'*. The late Paul Cannell, who was Creation's in-house artist, was asked to expand on the work that he did for *'Higher Than The Sun'*, altering the sun's colours and creating a piece of psychedelic work that was every bit as flamboyant as the released album. Created from house paints and car body filler, Cannell's work received the ultimate accolade in 2010 when it was chosen alongside nine other album covers, including *Park Life* and *London Calling*, for a set of stamps by Royal Mail that celebrated classic albums.

And *Screamadelica* really is a classic vinyl that's worth celebrating. Created when acid house was just

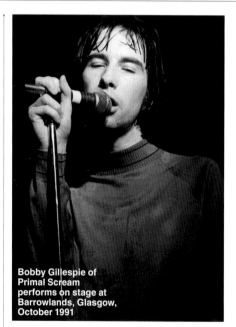

Bobby Gillespie of Primal Scream performs on stage at Barrowlands, Glasgow, October 1991

beginning to take off in the UK, Bobby Gillespie and the rest of the band were canny enough to know that it should embrace the rising club scene rather than ignore it. With that in mind, they enlisted the likes of Andrew Weatherall, The Orb, Hypnotone and The Rolling Stones' producer, Jimmy Miller, to produce numerous tracks, creating a distinctive sound that

not only helped the band move away from its original image, but proved that dance music and rock could coexist together and sound amazing doing so.

While *Screamadelica* was recently rereleased in 2015, original pressings are still plentiful and available at very reasonable prices, meaning that you are able to catch a band at the height of its powers and drink in that glorious cover for very little outlay.

Track List

SIDE A
Track 1: Movin' On Up
Track 2: Slip Inside This House
Track 3: Don't Fight It, Feel It
SIDE B
Track 1: Higher Than The Sun
Track 2: Inner Flight
Track 3: Come Together
SIDE C
Track 1: Loaded
Track 2: Damaged
Track 3: I'm Comin' Down
SIDE D
Track 1: Higher Than The Sun (A Dub Symphony In Two Parts)
Track 2: Shine Like Stars

Blue Lines

Massive Attack

Release Date: 1991 | **Record Label:** Coach House Studios, Bristol And Eastcote Studio/Wildbunch

Blue Lines' distinctive cover might well hint at the power of the music found within it, but it's also a subtle nod to a far older album, Stiff Little Fingers' *Inflammable Material.* As it turns out, Massive Attack's startling debut would draw inspiration from a number of unlikely sources, including concept albums by Pink Floyd, as well as artists as diverse as Isaac Hayes, Herbie Hancock and Public Image Ltd. The eclectic influences resulted in a fusion of reggae, hip hop, electronic music, dub and '70s soul that not only sounded like nothing else that was around at the time, but also led to the genesis of trip hop and helped make the world become aware of the Bristol sound, which included acts as diverse as Roni Size, Monk & Canatella and Portishead.

Released via Virgin on the group's own Wild Bunch label, work on *Blue Lines* lasted for roughly eight months, but several of its songs had been based on concepts that were up to seven years old. Neneh Cherry (who would score a writing credit on the album's final single, *'Hymn Of The Big Wheel'*, and sing backing vocals for it) also played a prominent role in the album's creation, allowing the trio to record parts of *Blue Lines* in her child's bedroom. While Massive Attack consisted of vocalist Grantley 'Daddy G' Marshall and keyboardists Robert '3D' Del Naja and

Massive Attack in 2003

Andrew 'Mushroom' Vowles, the trio was canny enough to surround itself with a number of key vocalists, including Horace Andy, Tony Bryan, Tricky, and Shara Nelson, whose rich, powerful voice features on several tracks, including the smash hit *'Unfinished Sympathy'*. The large range of contributors ensured that you never knew what to expect from *Blue Lines'* nine tracks, while the inclusion of live instruments ensured that it sounded notably different from the American hip hop that was popular at the time.

While *Blue Lines* was rereleased on vinyl in 2016, original pressings are still easily available and at decent prices, meaning that if you are a purist who prefers to listen to first prints, you'll be able to revisit Massive Attack's stunning debut without breaking the bank.

Track List

SIDE A
Track 1: Safe From Harm
Track 2: One Love
Track 3: Blue Lines
Track 4: Be Thankful For What You've Got
Track 5: Five Man Army
SIDE B
Track 1: Unfinished Sympathy
Track 2: Daydreaming
Track 3: Lately
Track 4: Hymn Of The Big Wheel

The Chronic

Dr Dre

Release Date: 1992 | **Record Label:** Death Row Records

To understand the significance — and widespread success — of hip-hop producer Andre 'Dr Dre' Young's first solo album, you need to grasp the evolution of hip-hop itself.

From its late-Seventies roots on the streets of New York until the mid-'80s, it was essentially party music. From around '87 onwards, gangsta rap from Ice-T and NWA attracted many listeners' attention, thanks to its shocking depictions of inter-gang violence and the

American rapper, record producer and entrepreneur, Dr Dre is still very much in the industry

racism embedded in America's police forces. By 1992, the music was changing once more, largely thanks to Public Enemy's intelligent rhymes and the phenomenal layers of sampled funk on this album, the first of the so-called G-Funk wave (note the play on words of P-Funk, or Parliament-Funkadelic, the band that supplied many of the sounds).

As a musician, Dre was a clever, inventive pioneer; as a person, however, he was an unreconstructed thug, having beaten up at least two women who dared to cross him in his early career as a member of NWA. These two aspects of his character neatly sum up *The Chronic*, which contains unbeatable swathes of sounds and amazing grooves, while focusing lyrically on violence, dope-smoking, and endless 'bitches'.

If you can get over the album's relentless misogyny and its juvenile obsession with a lifestyle of debauchery, you will enjoy the big hit '*Nuthin' but a 'G' Thang*', and several songs on which the young Snoop Dogg made his presence felt. Elsewhere, Dre vents his dislike of his fellow former NWA members Eazy-E and Ice Cube with homophobic insults; describes scenes from the Compton hood that are both grimly amusing and blood-soaked; and paints a picture of hatred and arrogance that gripped the attention of millions.

Lyrically confrontational, thematically controversial and musically brilliant, *The Chronic* paved the way for its creator towards major stardom. In the end, Dre's dubious personal history seemed to deter his fan base not a jot; two decades after *The Chronic*, their continued support of his music and business ventures had made him hip-hop's richest man.

Track List

SIDE A

Track 1:	The Chronic
Track 2:	Fuck Wit Dre Day (And Everybody'sCelebratin')
Track 3:	Let Me Ride
Track 4:	The Day The N****z Took Over
Track 5:	Nuthin' But A 'G' Thang
Track 6:	Deeez Nuuuts
Track 7:	Lil' Ghetto Boy

SIDE B

Track 1:	A N**** Witta Gun
Track 2:	Rat-Tat-Tat-Tat
Track 3:	The $20 Sack Pyramid
Track 4:	Lyrical Gangbang
Track 5:	High Powered
Track 6:	The Doctor's Office
Track 7:	Stranded On Death Row
Track 8:	The Roach
Track 9:	Bitches Ain't Shit

Slanted And Enchanted

Pavement

Release Date: 1992 | **Record Label:** Matador Records

Routinely hailed as one of the Nineties' best rock albums, Pavement's debut record Slanted And Enchanted isn't an easy listen — but it is a compelling one. Comparisons to The Fall are often made, and with good reason as the music is gritty, with trebly bass and drums that are hit rather than played. Pavement's similarity to the pioneering Mancunian post-punks doesn't stop there, either: both bands had a tendency to perform chaotic gigs that didn't make sense to any but the most devoted fans; their mercurial frontman eventually split and reformed the band; and they never did what anyone expected or wanted them to do.

Formed in Stockton, California, in 1989, Pavement was the work of singer/guitarist/songwriter Stephen Malkmus, guitarist Scott Kannberg, bassist Mark Ibold, and a variety of drummers. Together they made a sound made up of scratchy guitars, intoned or yelled vocals, and more or less 'indie' production values. Their albums became a little smoother as the years passed: Slanted And Enchanted was raw, exciting and fairly primitive in comparison. Songs such as 'No Life Singed Her' had plenty of energy though, and made for memorable live performances once word had spread that Pavement was certainly a band worth seeing.

Elsewhere on this album, highlights include 'Conduit For Sale!', an alternately quiet-loud-quiet affair with a nod to the slower end of American hardcore; 'Chelsey's Little Wrists', a bathroom-quality wailathon with gibberish vocals and what sounded like a tapped jam jar keeping time; and the majestic 'Loretta's Scars', a full-frequency guitar anthem that sounded as if it came close to making commercial sense.

The rest of the songs oozed perverse energy; it's obvious why college-rock fans flocked to see Pavement play live, and also why the band never made it anywhere near the big time. It was just too unorthodox — although that didn't mean the songs weren't good. A split in 1999 was followed 11 years later by a successful (if brief) reunion, and it's no surprise that the gigs were packed to the rafters.

Energetic songs made live performances memorable

Track List

SIDE A
Track 1: Summer Babe (Winter Version)
Track 2: Trigger Cut / Wounded-Kite At :17
Track 3: No Life Singed Her
Track 4: In The Mouth A Desert
Track 5: Conduit For Sale!
Track 6: Zürich Is Stained
Track 7: Chesley's Little Wrists

SIDE B
Track 1: Loretta's Scars
Track 2: Here
Track 3: Two States
Track 4: Perfume-V
Track 5: Fame Throwa
Track 6: Jackals, False Grails: The Lonesome Era
Track 7: Our Singer

Rage Against The Machine

Rage Against The Machine

Release Date: 1992 | **Record Label:** Epic

Funk-metal begat rap-metal, which begat nu-metal, and somewhere embedded in that process was Rage Against The Machine, a band that combined rapped and/or shouted vocals with the catchiest of guitar riffs, and reaped immense rewards. The foursome's confrontational attitude towards authority helped it gain a mostly teenage audience when its self-titled debut album appeared in 1992, while its alliance with a major record label — despite its socialist politics — led to criticism from older, more cynical rock fans.

For both of these reasons, Rage Against The Machine's fanbase has generally been confined to middle-class white kids, but those outside that demographic are missing out on a truly excellent album. You may or may not enjoy frontman Zack de la Rocha's splenetic rhymes, but there's no denying

the sincerity behind his anti-corporate, anti-racist lyrics — and as for the band, there has rarely been a tighter, more musically competent guitar, bass and drums trio in the entire rock canon. Guitarist Tom Morello is a master of his instrument, coaxing such unorthodox sounds from it that the band felt it appropriate to place a sticker on the LP sleeve that stated 'no samples, keyboards or synthesisers were used in the making of this record'. It's little wonder he went on to play with Bruce Springsteen when Rage Against the Machine went on hiatus from 2000 to 2007.

And the songs? A blast from start to finish, without a weak one among them. Rage's best-known song to this day is still *'Killing In The Name'*, which — with its infamous final shrieks of *"Fuck you, I won't do what you tell me!"* — is a stadium-igniting tune like no other. *'Bullet In The Head'*, with its anti-capitalist venom, and *'Wake Up'*, a vehement call to arms that soundtracked the 1999 sci-fi thriller The Matrix, are two other high points. The sum of these ten songs is far more than its parts, leaving us with an album that is simultaneously intelligent and aggressive. Subsequent Rage Against The Machine albums didn't quite match up to this sterling debut effort, but there's no shame in that.

Track List

SIDE A
Track 1: Bombtrack
Track 2: Killing In The Name
Track 3: Take The Power Back
Track 4: Settle For Nothing
Track 5: Bullet In The Head

SIDE B
Track 1: Know Your Enemy
Track 2: Wake Up
Track 3: Fistful Of Steel
Track 4: Township Rebellion
Track 5: Freedom

Rapper and vocalist Zack de la Rocha

RATM at Finsbury Park

Midnight Marauders

A Tribe Called Quest

Release Date: 1993 | **Record Label:** Jive

The Queens, New York, trio A Tribe Called Quest was, along with its fellow New York musicians De La Soul, part of a hip-hop collective known as the Native Tongues. In the late '80s, and for most of the '90s, these groups stood out from the miasma of conflicting styles within American hip-hop thanks to their mellow but persuasive beats; rhymes that were observational and positive rather than violent or feud-related, and samples that soothed rather than inflamed the listener.

A Tribe Called Quest had made an impact as early as 1990 with its single *'Can I Kick It?'*, which sampled a diverse range of sources such as Lou Reed's *'Walk On The Wild Side'* and the British children's TV series *SuperTed*. By 1993 and its third album, *Midnight Marauders*, the Tribe had refined its music still further,

Phife Dawg formed the band in 1985

including explicit social commentary such as *'Steve Biko (Stir It Up)'*, recorded in honour of the murdered South African activist; and *'Sucka N****'*, which discussed the usage of racial epithets.

These examples aside, on this record A Tribe Called Quest proudly explored a lyrically obscure world of its own. The dreamy flow of words on the album's biggest single — and indeed, by far the band's best-known song to this day — 'Award Tour' was complemented by the slick but always subtle musical textures that were laid down by the group. *'Electric Relaxation'*, too, sounded as its title would lead you to expect, saturated with smooth grooves from the catalogues of jazz and soul musicians Ramsey Lewis and Ronnie Foster. *'Oh My God'* featured a slick guest rap from Busta Rhymes, who was a couple of years away from success himself as a solo artist at the time; while Raphael Saadiq of the R&B group Tony! Toni! Toné! supplied an appropriately honeyed vocal on the track *'Midnight'*.

Much of the hip-hop and urban music released as long ago as 1993 has failed to stand the test of time, whether through the naivety of the rhymes or the tinny nature of the instrumentation. However, *Midnight Marauders* avoids both of these pitfalls thanks to its bass-heavy production, and the fact that there's not a gun or gang reference in sight.

Track List

SIDE A
Track 1: Midnight Marauders Tour Guide
Track 2: Steve Biko (Stir It Up)
Track 3: Award Tour
Track 4: 8 Million Stories
SIDE B
Track 1: Sucka N****
Track 2: Midnight
Track 3: We Can Get Down
SIDE C
Track 1: Electric Relaxation
Track 2: Clap Your Hands
Track 3: Oh My God
Track 4: Keep It Rollin'
SIDE D
Track 1: The Chase, Part II
Track 2: Lyrics to Go
Track 3: God Lives Through
Track 4: Hot Sex (Europe-only bonus track)

In Utero

Nirvana

Release Date: 1993 | Record Label: DGC

"*Teenage angst has paid off well, but now I'm tired and old.*" The opening line of Nirvana's third (and final) studio album, *In Utero*, immediately expresses a desire to depart from the polished sound of its 1991 predecessor, *Nevermind*. Following the astounding success of its breakthrough anthem *'Smells Like Teen Spirit'* in particular, Kurt Cobain found himself overwhelmed with and despising of the band's sudden stardom — a recurring theme of the album. Fearful of alienating its core fanbase, the band intended to produce a much more abrasive record, closer resembling the sound of debut album *Bleach*. Sadly, this was the last record released by the band before Cobain's suicide less than a year later, although compilation and live albums were issued posthumously.

After laying down early demos with Jack Endino, *Bleach*'s producer, *In Utero* was recorded over the course of two weeks at Pachyderm Studio in Minnesota, USA, towards the beginning of 1993. Responsible for recording two of Cobain's favourite

albums (*Surfer Rosa* by Pixies and The Breeders' *Pod*), Steve Albini was hired to produce the album for a flat rate of $100,000, despite previously dismissing the band as merely "REM with a fuzzbox," and "…an unremarkable version of the Seattle sound."

Shortly after recording wrapped up, rumours started to surface that Nirvana's record label, DGC, disliked the album and was apprehensive towards releasing it in its state. *'Heart-Shaped Box'*, *'Pennyroyal Tea'* and *'All Apologies'* were later remixed by REM producer Scott Litt, alongside minor tweaks being made to the original mix elsewhere on the record, creating friction between Albini and the band.

Of the 18 tracks the band took into the recording sessions, 12 made it onto the final album, albeit some with reworked titles: *'Punky New Wave Number'* (*'Very Ape'*), *'New Poopie'* (*'Tourette's'*), *'Nine Month Media Blackout'* (*'Radio Friendly Unit Shifter'*) and *'La La La: Alternateen Anthem'* (*'All Apologies'*) were just some of the alternate titles unused. Among the tracks that didn't

> **"Nirvana's record label, DGC, disliked the album and was apprehensive towards releasing it"**

Track List

SIDE A
- **Track 1:** Serve the Servants
- **Track 2:** Scentless Apprentice
- **Track 3:** Heart-Shaped Box
- **Track 4:** Rape Me
- **Track 5:** Frances Farmer Will Have Her Revenge on Seattle
- **Track 6:** Dumb

SIDE B
- **Track 1:** Very Ape
- **Track 2:** Milk It
- **Track 3:** Pennyroyal Tea
- **Track 4:** Radio Friendly Unit Shifter
- **Track 5:** Tourette's
- **Track 6:** All Apologies

Cobain and Novoselic at the 1992 MTV Video Music Awards

was the work of Robert Fisher, who had designed all of Nirvana's releases on DGC to this point. The reverse features a collage of plastic body parts and model foetuses on a bed of flowers created by Cobain on his living room floor, maintaining the sleeve's medical theme that reflects some of the record's lyrical content. Also included was an inner sleeve printed with lyrics and black-and-white band photography.

Despite a limited promotional campaign and quiet dismay from DGC, In Utero accrued 180,000 sales in its first week, went on to be certified 5x platinum, and has now sold 15 million copies worldwide. Original pressings of In Utero were cut in clear vinyl and limited to 15,000 copies in the US, and select other versions of the album feature hidden track 'Gallons of Rubbing Alcohol Flow Through the Strip'. The record has received a number of subsequent reissues across picture discs, unofficial coloured vinyls, double LP gatefolds, and as part of collector's boxsets. Notably in 2003, DGC's parent label, Geffen Records, released a vinyl reissue cut from different master tapes, widely accepted to be Albini's original, unaltered mix. In celebration of the album's 20th anniversary, a 3LP triple gatefold deluxe edition was released, featuring the entire album remastered over two discs at 45rpm and a 33 rpm disc of B-sides and rarities, all pressed on 180g heavyweight vinyl.

make the cut was 'Marigold', the only Nirvana song written by drummer Dave Grohl.

The album's title, In Utero, was taken from a line of poetry written by Cobain's wife, Courtney Love, after considering several alternatives during the record's production. Verse Chorus Verse and Sappy were two such suggestions, though Cobain originally wanted to wryly dub the LP 'I Hate Myself And I Want To Die' — his customary sarcastic response to 'How are you doing?'

The anatomical angel that adorns In Utero's cover

OTHER ALBUMS

Bleach (1989)
Recorded for only $606 (and it certainly shows) in 1989, Nirvana's pre-Grohl, rough-around-the-edges debut, Bleach, features standout tracks 'Blew', 'About a Girl' and a cover of Shocking Blue's 'Love Buzz'.

Nevermind (1991)
One of the most pivotal records of the '90s, Nevermind, and in particular 'Smells Like Teen Spirit', ushered in rock music's ascent. It was certified diamond in the United States, with 30 million copies sold worldwide.

MTV Unplugged In New York (1994)
Recorded just five months before Cobain's suicide, and released posthumously, this live LP captures Nirvana's genius underneath the fuzz and racket. It's a fascinating listen spanning its short-lived career.

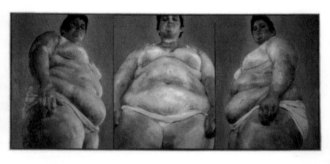

THE HOLY BIBLE
MANIC STREET PREACHERS

1. YES
2. IFWHITEAMERICATOLDTHETRUTHFORONEDAYIT'SWORLDWOULDFALLAPART
3. OF WALKING ABORTION • 4. SHE IS SUFFERING • 5. ARCHIVES OF PAIN
6. REVOL • 7. 4st 7lb • 8. MAUSOLEUM • 9. FASTER • 10. THIS IS YESTERDAY
11. DIE IN THE SUMMERTIME • 12. THE INTENSE HUMMING OF EVIL • 13. P.C.P.

The Holy Bible

Manic Street Preachers

Release Date: 1994 | Record Label: Epic

The Manic Street Preachers is a band that should be more famous than it is. Not only did it have number-one singles in the charts, but the band also took part in a concert in the Millennium Stadium, Wales, where it played the last song broadcasted around the world that century as part of the TV special *2000 Today*. Yet it still remains almost a cult band. The Manic Street Preachers' third album, *The Holy Bible*, was the last to feature lyricist and guitarist Richey Edwards, who was suffering from anorexia and depression, and would disappear months after the album was released. Much of what he was feeling and experiencing was put into the album's lyrics, leading to a darker tone than other Manics albums. For the fans it's either a love or hate album, but one thing cannot be argued: it remains a well-crafted album. The band moved away from its punk/hard-rock roots, and adopted more of a post-punk sound, although the single *Faster* displays a pure punk sound. The band was offered the chance to record *The Holy Bible* in Barbados, but decided to record in a small studio in Cardiff. The Manics is sometimes linked to the Britpop scene due to the success of its later singles, but it was far away from the scene when taking off, dressed in military clothing and playing a dark, grungier-sounding album. To promote the album, the Manics went on

Top of the Pops and played the single *'Faster'* while dressed in military clothing and balaclavas. The BBC reportedly received a record number of complaints — around 25,000. On its release, *The Holy Bible* was seen as a disappointment commercially, but praised by critics, and it has only grown in significance due to the events surrounding Richey Edwards. On the album's 20th anniversary, a special boxset was released that includes a remix of the whole album, which some fans consider to be superior to the original mix.

Manic Street Preachers, London 1994

Track List

SIDE A
Track 1: Yes
Track 2: Ifwhiteamericatoldthetruthfor onedayit'sworldwouldfallapart
Track 3: Of Walking Abortion
Track 4: She Is Suffering
Track 5: Archives Of Pain
Track 6: Revol
Track 7: 4st 7lb
SIDE B
Track 1: Mausoleum
Track 2: Faster
Track 3: This Is Yesterday
Track 4: Die In The Summertime
Track 5: The Intense Humming Of Evil
Track 6: P.C.P.

Illmatic

Nas

Release Date: 1994 | **Record Label:** Columbia

In the early '90s, West Coast rap was on the rise, with Death Row Records making Los Angeles the new place for hip hop.However, in 1994, Nas reestablished New York as the rap capital with *Illmatic*. Songs like *'N.Y. State Of Mind'* and *'The World Is Yours'* are staples in early '90s rap now, but Illmatic and its singles weren't commercial successes at the time. At only 20 years old when he released the debut album, Nas poetically described situations in ways that most rappers couldn't in their entire career. He grew up in the Queensbridge housing projects during the '80s and '90s, when there was a growing trend of crack use, and an increase in crime and violence that came with it. He rapped about the poverty and crime around him, never glorifying anything, leaving it to the listener to interpret what he was saying. Nas delivered his lyrics with flow, intensity and passion. This, along with the realness of his perspective, gave him a sense of credibility. The lyrics, as well as the simple album cover of seven-year-old Nas with Queensbridge imposed behind him, transports you to the time and place. In terms of the music, the instruments are kept simple and stay in the background, enabling the focus to stay on Nas's gritty lyrics.

At a time when each rapper had their own producer, Nas decided to use a number of well-renowned ones for *Illmatic*, with each adding to the music. The album doesn't suffer from having too many people's input, as the sound remains consistent. Nas is so natural with the microphone that on the first track, *'N.Y State Of Mind'*, when he says the line *"I don't know how to start this shit,"* it makes you believe that the lyrics that flow from Nas are genuinely coming from his mind then and there. On vinyl, the Side A and Side B are renamed to the 40th Side North and 41st Side South respectively, which are the streets that form the boundary that divide the Queensbridge housing projects. To mark 20 years since the release of the album, a two-LP special edition was released titled *Illmatic XX*. This edition on vinyl comes with the original ten songs as well as a download code for ten bonus tracks including unreleased demos and freestyles.

Nas in 1998

Track List

SIDE A
- **Track 1:** The Genesis
- **Track 2:** N.Y. State Of Mind
- **Track 3:** Life's A Bitch
- **Track 4:** The World Is Yours
- **Track 5:** Halftime

SIDE B
- **Track 1:** Memory Lane (Sittin' In Da Park)
- **Track 2:** One Love
- **Track 3:** One Time 4 Your Mind
- **Track 4:** Represent
- **Track 5:** It Ain't Hard To Tell

Definitely Maybe

Oasis

Release Date: 1994 | **Record Label:** Clear Studios, Manchester, The Pink Museum, Liverpool/Creation

Definitely Maybe's iconic album cover is filled with all manner of fascinating insights into its performers. The shot of *The Good, the Bad and the Ugly* is a nod to one of Noel Gallagher's favourite films; likewise, the photo of Burt Bacharach is a tribute to one of Noel's musical heroes and is also thought to be a sly nod to Pink Floyd's *Ummagumma*. There are also photos of George Best and Rodney Marsh, two of the most prominent football players to perform for Manchester United and Manchester City, respectively. And then of course there are the copious amounts of wine and cigarettes on display, an obvious nod to one of the most popular tracks on the album, *Cigarettes & Alcohol*. It's a glorious piece of photography that effortlessly sums up both Oasis and the '90s.

While *Definitely Maybe* shot to the top of the UK charts and became the fastest-selling UK debut of all time — it would eventually sell over 15 million copies — its conception was far from straightforward. Initial recordings with Dave Batchelor proved unsuccessful, while recordings at Cornwall's Sawmills Studio, this time with Noel producing alongside Mark Coyle, also failed to produce the desired effect. Owen Morris was eventually called in to salvage the recordings, mastering the album at Johnny Marr's personal studio. The end result remains Oasis' most exciting-sounding record, full of swagger and attitude, as if the very essence of the Gallaghers themselves was somehow captured within the double LP's grooves.

Definitely Maybe didn't just herald the arrival of the Gallaghers; it also helped to cement the arrival of Britpop that had been arguably kickstarted by misfits Suede, but was aggressively pursued by the likes of Blur, Elastica and Supergrass. The members of Oasis became as popular as their album, with the two brothers predictably absorbing most of the limelight. The popularity and success of *Definitely Maybe* probably helps to explain why original pressings can continually fetch over £100 on the second-hand market. Luckily, those with fewer pennies in their pocket can enjoy the rerelease that costs a fraction of the price.

Oasis, London 2008

Track List

SIDE A
Track 1: Rock 'N' Roll Star
Track 2: Shakermaker
Track 3: Live Forever
SIDE B
Track 1: Up In The Sky
Track 2: Columbia
Track 3: Sad Song
SIDE C
Track 1: Supersonic
Track 2: Bring It On Down
Track 3: Cigarettes & Alcohol
SIDE D
Track 1: Digsy's Dinner
Track 2: Slide Away
Track 3: Married With Children

Dave Hogan/Getty Images

Dummy

Portishead

Release Date: 1994 | **Record Label:** State of Art and Coach House Studios, Bristol/Go! Beat

Dummy's **cover is stark and unsettling.** The sombre image features a distraught-looking Beth Gibbons (Portishead's lead singer) sitting in solitude with an intravenous drip in her arm and makeup visibly running down her face. It's a harrowing portrait further amplified by its grubby image quality that looks like it has been shot with a low-resolution camera. The actual snapshot is taken from a short film called *To Kill a Dead Man*, which was written and scored by Gibbons, along with remaining Portishead members Geoff Barrow and Adrian Utley, and additional shots of the 11-minute spy caper can also be found on the vinyl's sleeve. It's an unconventional image to launch a new record, but unconventional is what sums up Portishead absolutely perfectly.

Portishead, Denmark 2011

Dummy's sound is as desolate and sombre as its iconic cover, delivering a tense and often film-like score, which sounded like nothing else around at the time of its release. Just like Massive Attack, Portishead was hugely influenced by American hip hop, but whereas *White Lines* veered towards soul and rap, Gibbons' distinctive vocals gave Portishead's debut a more folk-like feel. Of course it certainly helped that Barrow was extremely liberal with the album's sampling, freely borrowing snatches from film scores and the likes of Isaac Hayes in order to create an utterly unique wall of sound that is as diverse in its structure as it is haunting to listen to.

Barrow even went so far as to use vinyl scratching, which gave *Dummy's* CD release an incredibly distinctive sound, however, it is ironically lost on its vinyl outing, where you could be forgiven for thinking that you had a particularly noisy copy if you had never heard the album before.

Dummy's uniqueness not only earned it the 1995 Mercury Music Prize, but also saw it achieve sales of over 2 million in Europe, with the vast majority coming from the UK. Surprisingly, original pressings of *Dummy* can often be picked up for as little as £30, although purists may want to seek out the rarer Greek pressing that includes the excellent *It's A Fire*, which was never released on the original LP.

Track List

SIDE A
Track 1: Mysterons
Track 2: Sour Times
Track 3: Strangers
Track 4: It Could Be Sweet
Track 5: Wandering Star
SIDE B
Track 1: Numb
Track 2: Roads
Track 3: Pedestal
Track 4: Biscuit
Track 5: Glory Box

Felix Kunze/Redferns

Pulp Fiction

Various Artists

Release Date: 1994 | **Record Label:** MCA

Pulp Fiction's front cover is a phenomenal piece of work by James Verdesoto, effortlessly capturing the spirit of the old noir novels and pulp magazines that the film refers to. A sultry looking Uma Thurman is in character as the vampish Mia Wallace, a cigarette in one hand, her other resting atop a pulp fiction novel. The whole album cover has a wrinkled, weather-beaten look to it, while a ten-cents sticker adorns the top-right corner, again harking back to the popular pulp novels that rose to prominence during the '20s and '30s.

The soundtrack is every bit as dynamic as its cover, thanks to a masterful blending of carefully chosen lines of dialogue and songs that perfectly capture the key moments of Tarantino's movie. *Pulp Fiction* certainly wasn't the first time that Tarantino

Urge Overkill performs at the Catalyst on 23 April 1994 in Santa Cruz California

had pulled off this trick — the album accompanying *Reservoir Dogs* is similarly structured — but it's arguably more accomplished, and led to a spawn of imitators. The album was every bit as successful as the film, selling in its millions and bringing Urge Overkill worldwide acclaim thanks to its cover of Neil Diamond's *'Girl, You'll Be A Woman Soon'*, and a resurgence for Kool & the Gang. We can only imagine how many of the tracks would be littering the download charts if the film were released today.

There's a personality to *Pulp Fiction's* soundtrack that few other film soundtracks managed to replicate, with the 2014 release of *Guardians Of The Galaxy* being one of the most recent examples of a soundtrack that arguably captured the spirit of its source material. Tarantino's movie didn't have a traditional score, but it didn't need it, as its carefully picked tunes easily captured what was being portrayed on-screen. Like Martin Scorsese before him, Tarantino understands the power of music, and uses it perfectly.

Sadly, the later 2002 edition that featured four additional tracks and an interview with Tarantino never received a vinyl release, although there are a number of exclusive picture discs featuring the album's cover that are worth tracking down. It's otherwise easily available from most retailers.

Track List

SIDE A
Track 1a: Pumpkin And Honey Bunny
Track 1b: Misirlou
Track 2: Royale With Cheese
Track 3: Jungle Boogie
Track 4: Let's Stay Together
Track 5: Bustin' Surfboards
Track 6: Lonesome Town
Track 7: Son Of A Preacher Man

SIDE B
Track 1a: Jack Rabbit Slims Twist Content
Track 1b: You Never Can Tell
Track 2: Girl, You'll Be A Woman Soon
Track 3: If Love Is A Red Dress (Hang Me In Rags)
Track 4a: Bring Out The Gimp
Track 4b: Comanche
Track 5: Flowers On The Wall
Track 6: Personality Goes A Long Way
Track 7: Surf Rider
Track 8: Ezekiel 25:17

Superunknown

Soundgarden

Release Date: 1994 | **Record Label:** A&M

The late singer Chris Cornell was a man of many talents, quite apart from his unearthly vocal range. Prominent among them was his ability to write songs that fused hard rock with a pop-influenced melodic sensibility and present them to the masses with total conviction. It certainly helped that grunge, the Seattle sound in which his band — Soundgarden — emerged, was based on a blend of singable choruses, metal riffs and a sense of nihilistic doom, all of which suited the band's ethos perfectly.

Superunknown was Soundgarden's fourth album, and the one that brought it to the wider, non-grunge-worshipping world. Alongside Nirvana, Pearl Jam and to a certain extent Alice In Chains, Cornell and his bandmates transcended their niche in a way

that, for example, Tad, Mudhoney and the Melvins never managed to achieve. At least part of this was undoubtedly due to a single song, *'Black Hole Sun'*, a metallic bit of Beatles whimsy that was based on an impossibly catchy chord sequence in the chorus. Heavy-metal fans absolutely loved the song's downtuned grind; grungers totally admired its depressive lyrics; and MTV and rock radio were all over the song like a rash. "It turned into our *'Dream On',*" sighed guitarist Kim Thayil, referencing the huge, millstone-like power ballad from 1973 by Aerosmith.

Four more singles were released from *Superunknown* in 1994 and 1995, helping to push it to nine million unit sales and five platinum awards from the RIAA. Of these, *'Spoonman'* was the most easily digestible — a loose-limbed riff workout; and *'Fell On Black Days'* the most contemplative. Soundgarden covered a lot of songwriting ground on this album, and all of it with great skill.

The album turned out to be its swansong, at least in the group's first period of activity; after its next album, 1996's *Down On The Upside*, Soundgarden went on hiatus. A reunion in 2010 was progressing nicely until Cornell's suicide in May 2017 at the age of only 52, tragically depriving his bandmates, fans and the rest of us of his phenomenal talent.

The late Chris Cornell performing in December 2015

Track List

SIDE A
Track 1: Let Me Drown
Track 2: My Wave
Track 3: Fell On Black Days
Track 4: Mailman

SIDE B
Track 1: Superunknown
Track 2: Head Down
Track 3: Black Hole Sun

SIDE C
Track 1: Spoonman
Track 2: Limo Wreck
Track 3: The Day I Tried To Live
Track 4: Kickstand

SIDE D
Track 1: Fresh Tendrils
Track 2: 4th Of July
Track 3: Half
Track 4: Like Suicide
Track 5: She Likes Surprises (Bonus Track On Clear Vinyl LP)

dubnobasswithmyheadman

Underworld

Release Date: 1994 | **Record Label:** Junior Boy's Own

After a brief hiatus-of-sorts at the turn of the decade, and the addition of emerging DJ Darren Emerson, *dubnobasswithmyheadman* ushered in the reincarnation of Underworld. Often considered the debut of Underworld Mk2, the nine-track record borrows from a diverse pool of musical genres, pop culture and literature — Lou Reed's 1989 album *New York*, and the autobiography of American playwright Sam Shepard among a few influences often cited by core members Karl Hyde and Rick Smith. The unorthodox album title was a result of Smith misreading Hyde's handwriting on a cassette tape during the recording process.

The introduction of Emerson to the group brought with it a renewed focus on production, the subtleties of which are best appreciated on wax. Gone were the played-out pop clichés that propped up Underworld's previous albums, replaced instead by a pioneering take on techno, which proved a catalyst for electronic music's rise to prominence over the course of the '90s. Through the course of the record, the band's newfound freedom to blur genre boundaries and explore influences is apparent, most notably during *'Tongue's'* dreamy guitars and the reggae-tinged rhythms of 'M.E'.

Tomato, a design collective of which Hyde and Smith are affiliated, created *dubnobasswithmyheadman's* striking art, which differs slightly between the vinyl and CD releases. Featured among the monochrome miscellany of type are some of the record's track titles, as well as lyric excerpts that became part of its defining 1995 single, *'Born Slippy .NUXX)'*. Haphazard though the artwork may seem, the cut-and-paste approach to it perfectly echoes Hyde's lyrical style: beat poetry made up of short snatches of conversations and ear-catching phrases collected on Hyde's New York travels.

In 2014, to celebrate the record's 20th anniversary, *dubnobasswithmyheadman* received a reissue on 180g vinyl over two discs. Meticulously remastered by Smith at London's infamous Abbey Road Studios, the fresh release of Underworld's seminal LP serves as a reminder of how far the album's influence has spread, over two decades since its initial outing.

Underworld at Bluedot Festival 2016

Track List

SIDE A
Track 1: Dark & Long
Track 2: Mmm…Skyscraper I Love You
SIDE B
Track 1: Surfboy
Track 2: Spoonman
Track 3: Tongue
SIDE C
Track 1: Dirty Epic
Track 2: Cowgirl
SIDE D
Track 1: River Of Bass
Track 2: M.E.

Timeless

Goldie

Release Date: 1995 | **Record Label:** FFRR Records

A couple of decades after the British songwriter Clifford 'Goldie' Price released his first full-length album, he did so much — remixing other musicians' music; acting in films, participating in dignity-free, reality-TV shows, such as S*trictly Come Dancing* and *The Jump*; being a talking head on TV — that it's hard to recall a time when he was only known for making jungle (as laymen called it) or drum and bass (the term that professionals used). In fact, all the other stuff that Goldie has done has rather got in the way of his solo discography, which only extends to a handful of albums in 20 years and counting. Of these, *Timeless* is the only classic; 1998's *Saturnz Return* had its

moments, not least an hour-long opening track, but it lacked the focus and sheer courage of its predecessor.

The title track, plus the big hit *'Inner City Life'*, were available on the CD version and the single LP, but not on the double LP, so those particular vinyl owners will have missed out. Still, the essential elements of those songs — sweet female vocals courtesy of the late Diane Charlemagne, frantic breakbeats, and trippy layers of backing synth — appeared on many of the other cuts.

The songs *'Kemistry'* — named after the DJ with whom Goldie had been in a previous relationship — and *'Angel'* bear a refreshingly light touch for a genre of music so focused on ear-bleeding tempos and battering-ram percussion, although serious intensity is available via pavement-cracking bass. It's this ability to switch from heavy to mellow at just a moment's notice that makes *Timeless* so entertaining.

Although drum and bass is now music for clubbers rather than for the mainstream audience, as it was until it peaked around 2001, Timeless has aged well. The sheer weight of the rhythms prevents them from sounding tinny (compare them with any mid-'90s house music and you'll see what we mean), while the elastic vocals are ageless. The entire drum-and-bass movement never got better than this album, in whichever format you choose to buy it.

Timeless was Goldie's first studio album, and entered the UK charts at #7

Track List

SIDE A
Track 1: Saint Angel
Track 2: This Is A Bad
SIDE B
Track 1: Kemistry (V.I.P Mix)
Track 2: You & Me
SIDE C
Track 1: Still Life
Track 2: Still Life (V.I.P Mix)
(The Latino Dego In Me)
SIDE D
Track 1: Jah the Seventh Seal
Track 2: A Sense Of Rage (Sensual V.I.P Mix)

OK Computer
Radiohead

Release Date: 1997 | **Record Label:** Parlophone/Capitol

Thom Yorke certainly isn't a man to mince his words. In an interview with Vox he expressed his disdain for *OK Computer's* cover, which had been created by long-time Radiohead collaborator Stanley Donwood. "It's pretty dreadful, but it's the best we could come up with at the time. But it's awful, I hate it, it's fucking rubbish." To us, it's not really a fair assessment, as *OK Computer's* cover design proved to be every bit as experimental as Radiohead's third album. Donwood began working on the startling cover early on in the production of *OK Computer*, slowly adjusting it over time. Wanting to create a bleached-bone look, Donwood created his piece of work using a tablet and a light pen. The only proviso? He wasn't allowed to erase anything. It sounds like madness, but the end result is a wonderfully abstract piece of work that proved to be just as eye-catching as his previous work on *The Bends* (he would go on to design all of Radiohead's later covers, including the latest album, *A Moon Shaped Pool*). Donwood's magnificent work

> **"There were concerns that there was nothing on the album that would match radio-friendly hit 'Creep'"**

continues to the back cover and the two sleeves, with the gatefold being used to house the album's progressive and sometimes depressing lyrics. One of the most interesting anecdotes about the cover's creation came about in early 2017, when a fan on Reddit noticed that the featured motorway appears identical to an intersection found in Hartford, Connecticut, with the photo possibly taken while the band was staying at the nearby Hilton Hotel.

Named after a line from *The Hitchhiker's Guide To The Galaxy*, and part-recorded in the supposedly haunted St Catherine's Court, Yorke claimed ghosts spoke to him in his sleep in a recent Rolling Stone interview. *OK Computer's* inspiration came from a number of different sources, including *Pet Sounds* by The Beach Boys, Miles Davis' *Bitches Brew*, and the dislocation Yorke felt from the non-stop touring the band was doing in America. The end result is an album that is rife with dour, miserable lyrics or songs based around uncomfortable themes. Final single *'Airbag'* was inspired by a car crash that Yorke was involved with

Track List

SIDE A
Track 1: Airbag
Track 2: Paranoid Android
Track 3: Subterranean Homesick Alien
SIDE B
Track 1: Exit Music (For A Film)
Track 2: Let Down
Track 3: Karma Police
SIDE C
Track 1: Fitter Happier
Track 2: Electioneering
Track 3: Climbing Up The Walls
Track 4: No Surprises
SIDE D
Track 1: Lucky
Track 2: The Tourist

Radiohead at Madison Square Garden

in 1987, while *'No Surprises'* discusses *"A job that slowly kills you"* and *"Bruises that won't heal."* The distinctive sound of *OK Computer* sent alarm bells ringing at Capitol, with sales projections changed from two million units to half a million, and there were concerns that there was nothing on the album that would match the radio-friendly hit *'Creep'*, which had helped catapult Radiohead to fame in 1992. Ultimately, Capitol's fears were unfounded, with *OK Computer* not only going on to sell over six million copies, but also drastically expanding the band's international audience. No stranger to critical acclaim on its release, the album continues to pull accolades, and constantly appears in many 'greatest albums' lists. It is seen by many as not only heralding the end of Britpop, but also inspiring a new generation of musicians, including Travis, Secret Machines and Bloc Party. It also marked a slight change in direction of Radiohead itself, with the band continuing to write experimental music that would further distance itself from its peers and help turn it into a worldwide phenomenon.

Released in the late '90s, original pressings of *OK Computer* can often reach high prices online, but it typically sells for around the £80 mark. Fortunately, there are numerous other alternatives for those with a little less cash. Emi released a reissue in 2008, while XL Recordings released its own pressing in 2016. Perhaps the most desirable version of the album, however, was released earlier this year in the form of *OK Computer OKNOTOK 1997 — 2017*. Spread across three LPs, it not only features remastered tracks, but also eight remastered B-sides, three previously unreleased tracks, a hardcover art book, and numerous other goodies. It's arguably the definitive version of a pretty definitive album, and should be in any serious collector's library.

OTHER ALBUMS

The Bends (1995)
Radiohead's second album received far more critical acclaim than its debut, *Pablo Honey*, did, and was bolstered by five hit singles, including *'Fake Plastic Trees'* and the epic *'Street Spirit (Fade Out)'*.

Kid A (2000)
Radiohead moved in new musical directions for its fourth album, and embraced synthesisers, string orchestras and drum machines. Radiohead would continue to push creatively with varying degrees of success.

In Rainbows (2007)
Radiohead's seventh studio album sent shockwaves through the industry when the band announced its pay-what-you-want scheme for the self-released album, which was absolutely unheard of at the time.

The Fragile
Nine Inch Nails

Release Date: 1999 | Record Label: Nothing/Interscope

In the buildup to the release of *The Fragile*, **fans didn't know what to expect.** Nine Inch Nails' singer Trent Reznor saying it sounded ridiculous didn't help. *The Fragile* is often compared to Pink Floyd's *The Wall*, a double album that explores isolation and depression and has a prog-rock vibe.

While there was a hint of the industrial sound from previous albums such as *The Downward Spiral*, Trent evolved the overall sound to include layers of ambient noises, pushing the genre towards more art rock as opposed to the alternate rock of Nine Inch Nails' previous works. The opening track, *'Somewhat Damaged'*, made the news when it was reported to be one of 13 songs used by the CIA at Guantanamo Bay played to detainees as a means of torture.

Trent Reznor, always one to alter his songs or albums after their release, made a few changes in the vinyl version of *The Fragile*. The album on vinyl consists of three LPs; each comes in a black sleeve with the word 'Nothing' printed on it. It also has two additional tracks not available on the CD version, *'10 Miles High'* and *'The New Flesh'*. A number of tracks were lengthened, while *'Ripe'* was shortened. In total the vinyl version is almost two hours long. There is also a four-LP version titled *The Fragile: Deviations 1*, which is made up of instrumentals and alternate versions of tracks on the regular version, as well as tracks recorded during the making of *The Fragile* but didn't make the final cut. If you have the time, the record has a total playtime of two and a half hours. For the regular-edition vinyl, as well as *Deviations 1*, you will be looking to spend over £150 for an opened copy, and over four times that for a sealed one.

Track List

SIDE A
Track 1: Somewhat Damaged
Track 2: The Day The World Went Away
Track 3: The Frail
Track 4: The Wretched

SIDE B
Track 1: We're In This Together
Track 2: The Fragile
Track 3: Just Like You Imagined
Track 4: Even Deeper

SIDE C
Track 1: Pilgrimage
Track 2: No, You Don't
Track 3: La Mer
Track 4: The Great Below

SIDE D
Track 1: The Way Out Is Through
Track 2: Into The Void
Track 3: Where Is Everybody?
Track 4: The Mark Has Been Made

SIDE E
Track 1: 10 Miles High
Track 2: Please
Track 3: Starfuckers, Inc.
Track 4: Complication
Track 5: The New Flesh

SIDE F
Track 1: I'm Looking Forward To Joining You, Finally
Track 2: The Big Come Down
Track 3: Underneath It All
Track 4: Ripe

Nine Inch Nails at the Zenith

The Soft Bulletin

Flaming Lips

Release Date: 1999 | **Record Label:** Warner Bros.

The Flaming Lips at VEGA in Copenhagen

The Flaming Lips received some radio playtime when its single *'She Don't Use Jelly'* charted in 1993, but the success went as quickly as it came.

The band's guitarist, Ronald, left a few years later, which led the band members to think about changing things up, starting with their sound, and they chose to do this by not getting a new guitarist. This change led to the album *Zaireeka*, an album of four CDs that were intended to be played all at the same time to create a stereo sound. *The Soft Bulletin* was written and recorded around the same time as *Zaireeka*. It might sound like a cliché, but you'll never hear an album like *The Soft Bulletin*: symphonic art rock with a lot of melancholy and layering of sound. The Flaming Lips wrote it with the impression that if it failed then the record label would drop them, so as a last hurrah they went all out.

The Soft Bulletin is often compared to Beach Boys' *Pet Sounds*. Both bands had distanced themselves from what they had done before to make a more orchestral album with a lot of layering of sounds and a more serious tone in lyrics. The album was impossible to re-create live as a band, and it would be incredibly expensive to play as it would need to hire musicians, so the band decided that it would have pre-recorded parts in place of instruments. However, to enhance the live performances, audience members could pick up receivers with headphones at the venues, and a transmitter would broadcast the performance to them, so they could hear everything perfectly while still feeling the music through the live sound system in the building.

The image on the album's sleeve came from a photo shoot used in a *Life* magazine article on LSD in 1966. Singer Wayne Coyne chose it, as he felt that the music fitted the image.

Track List

SIDE A
Track 1: Race For The Prize
Track 2: A Spoonful Weighs A Ton
Track 3: The Spark That Bled
Track 4: The Spiderbite Song

SIDE B
Track 1: Buggin'
Track 2: What Is The Light?
Track 3: The Observer

SIDE C
Track 1: Waitin' For A Superman
Track 2: Suddenly Everything Has Changed
Track 3: The Gash

SIDE D
Track 1: Slow Motion
Track 2: Feeling Yourself Disintegrate
Track 3: Sleeping On The Roof

'OOS

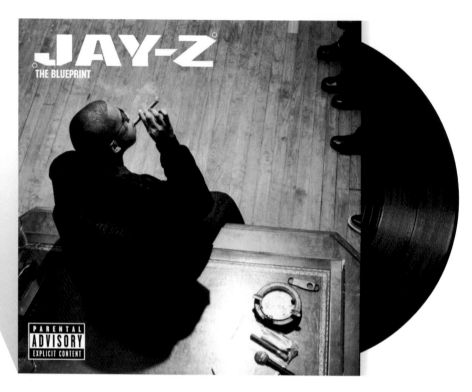

The Blueprint

Jay-Z

Release Date: 2001 | **Record Label:** Roc-A-Fella/Def Jam

In the half decade between *Reasonable Doubt* and *The Blueprint*, Shawn Carter the rapper became Jay-Z the mogul.

But after years of hustling and laying the groundwork for a musical empire, what happens when you finally emerge on top? When all the self-mythologising has actually come to pass, what's left to do, besides weep, for there are no more worlds to conquer? As it happens, it's precisely when on top that Jay-Z is most at home. *The Blueprint* suggests an outline, a sketch — it's anything but. Opening track, *'The Ruler's Back'*, is the ribbon cutting and everything that follows is a tour through Jay's grand design.

The tone throughout is celebratory, valedictory. Gone are the street-level sketches of albums past, replaced entirely with tracks befitting the greatest rapper living. Jay laughs off haters on the imperious *'Heart of the City'*, preaches his own enduring realness on *'Never Change'*, and spells out his fabulous wealth in black and white on *'U Don't Know'*, just in case it wasn't already abundantly clear. 'Put me anywhere on God's green earth, I'll triple my worth' sounds like typical rap braggadocio until you realise that it's less a boast, and more a statement of fact Behind the glass there's a wealth of talent, with a handful of producers putting their stamp on *The Blueprint's* soul-sampling style. Bink and Just Blaze lend their tracks a cinematic grandeur and soulful sensuality respectively, while Timbaland makes his sole appearance count with the Cuban-flavoured funk of *'Hola' Hovito'*. But it's a young Roc-A-Fella producer by the name of Kanye West who makes the most telling contributions. Just try getting that *'I Want You Back'* sample on *'Izzo (H.O.V.A.)'* out of your head.

The Blueprint is also a reminder of the heyday of hip-hop beef, when egos clashed over bars and beats rather than shade-throwing Instagram posts and Twitter feeds. *'Takeover'* is the album's monumental dis track, where over four verses of merciless barbs, snipes and outright dismissals, Jay picks apart Mobb Deep's Prodigy and, most infamously, Nas with brutal efficiency. *'Takeover'* might not have ended Nas' career — it arguably

> "The Blueprint is also a reminder of the heyday of hip-hop beef, when egos clashed over bars and beats"

Track List

SIDE A

Track 1:	The Ruler's Back
Track 2:	Takeover
Track 3:	Izzo (H.O.V.A.)
Track 4:	Girls, Girls, Girls
Track 5:	Jigga That N****
Track 6:	U Don't Know
Track 7:	Hola' Hovito
Track 8:	Heart Of The City (Ain't No Love)
Track 9:	Never Change
Track 10:	Song Cry
Track 11:	All I Need
Track 12:	Renegade
Track 13:	Blueprint (Momma Loves Me)

Few could argue against his raw and pure talent

boosted it given the reception to his infamous response, 'Ether' — but it remains a classic of the genre, and it's closing lines are still painfully withering: *"And all you other cats throwin' shots at Jigga/You only get half a bar — fuck y'all n****s."* Rivals vanquished, humiliated, cast aside, Jay takes the time to inhabit the various aspects of his kingpin persona. He's the player supreme on *'Girls, Girls,*

Girls' (we're still a couple of years removed from *'03 Bonnie & Clyde'* and *'Crazy In Love'* here). On *'Song Cry'* he plays the sensitive thug to perfection over Just Blaze's luxurious beat. And on *'All I Need'* he's the materialistic CEO, reeling off assets and achievements like the world's most ostentatious statement of account.

Only once does Jay deign to let another rapper take the mic, but then it's difficult for anyone to deny Marshall Mathers-era Eminem. The world's two biggest MCs circa 2001 trade bars on *'Renegade'* over a haunting Shady production that gets the best out of both of them. Both Jay and Em were arguably never better than at this particular moment in time, and to hear them railing against their detractors across the industry and the media on the same track is breathtaking stuff.

With the benefit of hindsight, it's easy to see *The Blueprint* as a peak, even though Hov continues to put out hit records pushing 50. It's the unmistakable sound of a man at the top of his game, one with nothing left to prove — not a bid to claim the throne, but a coronation. Maybe the most telling assessment comes from Jay himself: *"If I ain't better than Big, I'm the closest one,"* he says, invoking his idol in a moment of self-reflection. Few could argue against him. All hail the king.

The Blueprint is a reminder of the hip-hop heydays

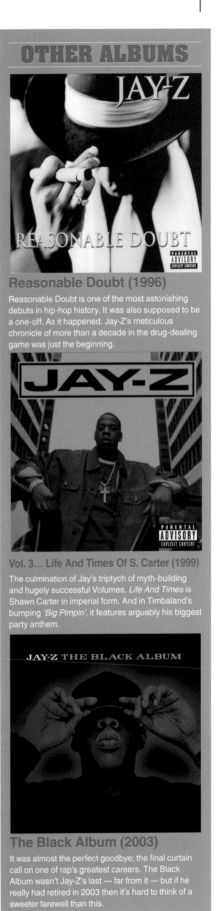

OTHER ALBUMS

Reasonable Doubt (1996)

Reasonable Doubt is one of the most astonishing debuts in hip-hop history. It was also supposed to be a one-off. As it happened, Jay-Z's meticulous chronicle of more than a decade in the drug-dealing game was just the beginning.

Vol. 3... Life And Times Of S. Carter (1999)

The culmination of Jay's triptych of myth-building and hugely successful Volumes, *Life And Times* is Shawn Carter in imperial form. And in Timbaland's bumping *'Big Pimpin'*, it features arguably his biggest party anthem.

The Black Album (2003)

It was almost the perfect goodbye; the final curtain call on one of rap's greatest careers. The Black Album wasn't Jay-Z's last — far from it — but if he really had retired in 2003 then it's hard to think of a sweeter farewell than this.

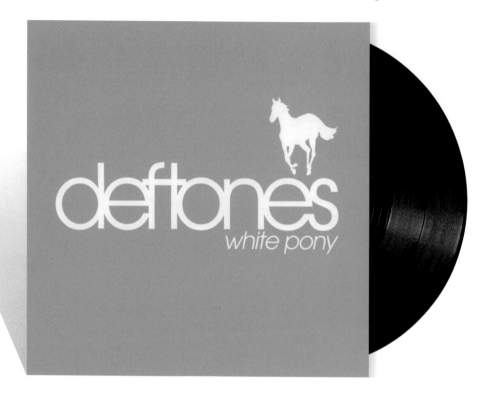

White Pony

Deftones

Release Date: 2000 | Record Label: Maverick

At the time of *White Pony's* release Nu-metal was in full flow with bands like Papa Roach, Limp Bizkit and Linkin Park in the charts, and, while other metal and hard rock bands at the time jumped on the trend, Deftones went in a different direction.

Though the band had a heavy sound, due to the low-tuned guitars of the genre, they opted for a more mellow and ambient sound. The track *'Change (In The House Of Flies)'* is a perfect example of this change, with haunting vocals and dark ambient sounds played in the background.

Deftones added a fifth member to their lineup, Frank Delgado, who had contributed parts on the previous two albums, but on *White Pony* he became a full-time member playing turntables and synths, adding to the electronic aspect of the sound. Singer Chino Moreno picked up the guitar when writing the album, this caused friction between him and the guitarist Stephen Carpenter but eventually led to a better album as the two tried to outdo each other when writing songs.

Drugs and violence are the key themes, with the name of the album being a reference to methamphetamine use or cocaine. Moreno chose not to sing about anything personal on the record, he chose instead to write stories and then lyrics to tell it. *'Digital Bath'*, for example, is about a man killing a woman by electrocuting her while she is in a bath. A limited edition version of the album was released in a red plastic sleeve which includes an extra track and comes on two clear red LPs, but this was limited to 1,000 copies. This version goes for between £200-300 when auctioned online.

Big Day Out, Gold Coast, 2014

Track List

SIDE A
Track 1: Feiticeira
Track 2: Digital Bath
Track 3: Elite
SIDE B
Track 1: RX Queen
Track 2: Street Carp
Track 3: Teenager
SIDE C
Track 1: Knife Prty
Track 2: Korea
Track 3: Passenger
SIDE D
Track 1: Change
Track 2: Pink Maggit

THE STROKES IS THIS IT

Is This It

The Strokes

Release Date: 2001 | **Record Label:** RCA/Rough Trade

In 2001, the rock charts received an influx of nu-metal bands such as **Linkin Park, Papa Roach and Slipknot, mainstream audiences wanted some traditional rock bands back on the radio.** The Strokes took influence from '70s rock sounds and gave it new life with the album *Is This It*. It was punk rock in everything but sound, The Strokes didn't want to record in a modern studio and decided to do it from dingy basement. They wanted the album to sound like a band from years past, so they would record as a band, rather than record parts separately, and only play it through the once.

Before the album was released, music magazine NME gave away free mp3 downloads of the song *'Last Nite'* and shortly afterwards they would put the band on the cover of their June 2001 issue claiming their music would change the readers lives. And they weren't far off. After its release, the album influenced a number of garage rock bands in the UK such as The Libertines and Arctic Monkeys. It is also credited towards turning record label's attention towards other garage rock bands in the States such as The Killers, Kings of Leon and The Black Keys.

There are differences between the US and international versions of the album. Due to the 9/11 attacks, the song *'New York City Cops'* was replaced in the US version with *'When It Started'*. The cover also differs between the US and international release, the picture of a nude woman's hip with a leather-glove resting on it was deemed too controversial for the American audience and an image of particle tracks was chosen as a replacement. In 2014 a limited edition Blue and Gold vinyl was released with a run of only 1,000 copies.

The Strokes at Petty Fest 2016

Track List

SIDE A
Track 1: Is This It
Track 2: The Modern Age
Track 3: Soma
Track 4: Barely Legal
Track 5: Someday
SIDE B
Track 1: Alone, Together
Track 2: Last Nite
Track 3: Hard To Explain
Track 4: New York City Cops
Track 5: Trying Your Luck
Track 6: Take It Or Leave It

Lateralus

Tool

Release Date: 2001 | **Record Label:** Volcano Entertainment

There is no band like Tool, and there is no album like the American alternative metallers' third LP, *Lateralus*, released after a five-year hiatus in which the group had progressed in their weird, often occult philosophy to the point where they were operating on a different plane to most other musicians. Read on and learn... *'Schism'*, the first single, is driven by a superbly dexterous bass-line from Justin Chancellor and was accompanied by a seriously disturbing video clip. Using a mixture of live action and claymation, the clip features bald, naked people in body paint performing bizarre, slow-motion acrobatics, levitating and sinking through the floor of a monochrome, sporadically-lit set. A red, tentacle-like plant slowly emerges from the neck of one of these figures; they walk on all fours, nodding their heads, like some strange nightmare creature. A cubic sector of brain is pulled slowly out of one character's head, and the camera zooms inside it, revealing that a spidery, predatory biped lurks within. Once released, this claymation animal — an eyeless humanoid with teeth and spindly limbs — runs across the floor and multiplies, with its offspring biting into the faces of the other humans and hanging from them. The clips ends with close-ups of a rotating ball of flames.

Now translate this to music, and you have the essence of this mind-blowing album.

Other highlights include the opening track, *'The Grudge'*, which is made up of several merged sections, including an ethereally beautiful bass arpeggio from Chancellor. Singer Maynard James Keenan advises the listener to let go and be transformed in the lyrics, which are sung in tones varying from subtle and staccato to a full-blown scream which endures for a minute or so at the song's end.

'Mantra' is a minute's worth of slow, echoed dolphin or whale noises — or so it seems. Keenan is said to have told a Japanese magazine in 2001 that he was squeezing one of his Siamese cats when the animal started making a moaning noise, presumably in pleasure. He fetched a recorder, captured the

> **"Maynard James Keenan advises the listener to let go and be transformed in the lyrics of the song"**

Track List

SIDE A
Track 1: The Grudge
Track 2: Eon Blue Apocalypse
Track 3: The Patient
Track 4: Mantra

SIDE B
Track 1: Schism
Track 2: Parabol
Track 3: Parabola
Track 4: Disposition

SIDE C
Track 1: Ticks And Leeches
Track 2: Lateralus

SIDE D
Track 1: Reflection
Track 2: Triad
Track 3: Faaip De Oiad

Their songs were intelligent collections of sequences and mathematical genius

feline's unusual utterances for posterity and slowed the sound right down in the studio. It's a good story, true or otherwise.

'Parabola' is a beefed-up rock anthem with a choir-like effect on some of Keenan's vocals. The singer delivers a paean to physical contact, telling a tale of two intertwined bodies whose pain is merely an illusion: the guitars and bass rage around him, before breaking down into a huge, doomy riff that is apocalyptic compared to the rest of the song.

But we're just getting started. The album's title track is one of its most ambitious. As the years have passed, information about its structure have been revealed which only a reasonably advanced and observant listener would have picked up on first spin. For starters, a large part of it is based on a repeating sequence of time signatures — 9/8, 8/8 and 7/4 — which form 987, the song's original title.

Then, examine Maynard's lyrics. You'll notice that the number of syllables of the words he sings between pauses are either 1, 1, 2, 3, 5, 8 and back down to 1, or 1, 1, 2, 3, 5, 8, 13 and back. These are the numbers of the Fibonacci sequence, a series which equates to the proportions of a spiral and which is found on innumerable occasions in nature, from the shape of galaxies to the structure of fern leaves. Furthermore, Keenan starts singing at one minute and 37 seconds into the song, which equates to 1:618 minutes: 1:618 is the famed 'golden ratio', a mathematical constant based on the relationship between two quantities, which has been the subject of much study since the ancient Greeks.

Like we said, there is no other band like Tool. A fourth album called 10,000 Days was released in 2006: although they have played live dates since then, there has been little sign of more new music from this unique band. The world definitely needs more of this stuff...

The is certainly no other band quite like Tool

Undertow (1993)
Tool debuted with an album that was compelling in parts, although it lacked the massive themes of their later albums and was aimed squarely at the alternative metal crowd. The big hits 'Sober' and 'Prison Sex' were astounding.

Aenima (1996)
The other truly essential Tool album is Aenima, where the band began to explore the wiring behind the existential motherboards on a deeper, more questioning level. 'Stinkfist' outraged MTV, who assumed it referred to sexual practices.

10,000 Days (2006)
The pressure of following up the immense Lateralus might have been a little much for the band. That being said, 'Vicarious' and 'The Pot' are as enjoyably weird as anything that they've ever recorded.

Songs For The Deaf

Queens Of The Stone Age

Release Date: 2002 | **Record Label:** Interscope

The album helped Queens Of The Stone Age break away from the niche of stoner-rock and into the wider world of chart-topping hard rock. *Songs for the Deaf* is a concept album, taking the listener on a drive along a desert in California through all the radio stations across the state. In between some tracks are skits as radio DJs talk introducing the next song, some may find these intrusive but they're scarce and don't last longer than a minute. The album opens with an engine starting up and tuning through the stations before going into the first song *'You Think I Ain't Worth A Dollar, But I Feel Like A Millionaire'*. The album features a number of guest musicians, but the most notable is Foo Fighters member and former drummer of Nirvana Dave Grohl on drums.

Their third album mixed elements from the previous two, with hard, pounding rock and melodic, trance-inspired grunge, but they tightened everything up to make a more consistent record. The single *'No One Knows'* earned them a lot of radio time, but they remember their roots with songs like *'A Song For The Dead'*, which showcase a more desert rock feel with its fuzzy guitars and raspy vocals with melodic backing.

The US version of the vinyl has its own album artwork and comes on two red LPs and has an exclusive track, a cover of Roky Erickson's *'Bloody Hammer'*. The UK vinyl has the CD artwork but with the colours reversed. There was also a limited edition EU version, which had two glow-in-the-dark LPs. The prices vary, but you will be looking to spend in the hundreds for them.

Track List

SIDE A

Track 1:	You Think I Ain't Worth A Dollar, But I Feel Like A Millionaire
Track 2:	No One Knows
Track 3:	First It Giveth
Track 4:	A Song For The Dead

SIDE B

Track 1:	The Sky Is Fallin'
Track 2:	Six Shooter
Track 3:	Hangin' Tree
Track 4:	Go With The Flow
Track 5:	Gonna Leave You

SIDE C

Track 1:	Do It Again
Track 2:	God Is In The Radio
Track 3:	Another Love Song

SIDE D

Track 1:	A Song For The Deaf
Track 2:	Mosquito Song

Queens of the Stoneage at Reading Festival

Sea Change

Beck

Release Date: 2002 | **Record Label:** Geffen

A lot had changed for Beck between 1999's *Midnite Vultures* and 2002's *Sea Change*. After ending a nine-year relationship just before his 30th birthday, Beck took a more reflective approach to writing songs and decided to write about his experience with most of the songs themes being loneliness and heartbreak. The eclectic styles of sounds like folk/funk/hip-hop/alternate rock that fans had come to expect from a Beck album was changed for acoustic ballads. The unusual and experimental songs were nowhere to be heard and what fans got was a more sombre emotion record. Quirkiness replaced with sincerity, synthesisers take a back seat to an acoustic guitar and hip-hop rapping was gone in favour of quiet melancholy.

Beck would usually write a song and put it aside for a while before coming back to it but with *Sea Change* the majority of songs were written in a week and then within a year they were taken to a studio. Beck's father, helped out during recording by arranging the string sections in the album. A divisive album for Beck fans, those who understand that story behind the album, and what he was going through, can enjoy the album on a personal level, while others simply see *Sea Change* as not what they wanted from Beck.

On Record Store Day 2012 a limited edition of *Sea Change* was released on a pink vinyl, if you want to buy this record expect to pay more than £250. Sadly, no Beck album has felt as personal and complete as *Sea Change*.

Beck performs at the O2 Academy in Brixton, London

Track List

SIDE A
Track 1: The Golden Age
Track 2: Paper Tiger
Track 3: Guess I'm Doing Fine
SIDE B
Track 1: Lonesome Tears
Track 2: Lost Cause
Track 3: End Of The Day
SIDE C
Track 1: It's All In Your Mind
Track 2: Round The Bend
Track 3: Already Dead
SIDE D
Track 1: Sunday Sun
Track 2: Little One
Track 3: Side Of The Road

Think Tank

Blur

Release Date: 2003 | Record Label: Parlophone

I t's not every band that could drastically move away from their established sound and still be successful. But Blur's album *13* could not have gone further away form the band's Britpop sound, the bright and poppy sound of *Parklife* and *The Great Escape* was replaced with a darker sound influenced by psychedelic and electronic music. *Think Tank* took the sound form *13* and added World music to their influences, making it into more of an art rock album.

Each member of Blur started to work on their own projects, the band's guitarist Graham Coxon released a number of solo albums, Bassist Alex James worked with the band Fat Les and singer Damon Albarn created the animated band Gorillaz and their debut album was incredibly successful. After coming back together to work on a new album, Coxon left the band after failing to make it to recording sessions and it was reported that he was dealing with alcoholism and depression. His absence is felt in the songs as the album is not guitar driven like the other records, instead

atmospheric world music and electronic sounds take the place of the musician. The only time Coxon's playing can be heard is on the closing track *'Battery In Your Leg'* and his guitar sounds almost haunting as it could be heard as a farewell. *'Sweet Song'* was reportedly written and recorded as Coxon and the band were in negotiations on Coxon's split from Blur. Damon Albarn lyrics *"And now it seems that we're falling apart, But I hope I see the good in you come back again, I just believed in you"* tells of how he felt at the time of the split.

Those who may know the band from singles *'Song 2'* or *'Parklife'* may be thrown off by what they hear. The album's sound would feature more electronic sounds in the forefront due to their lead guitarists departure but they also experimented with other instruments. Who would have thought we would hear a saxophone solo in a Blur song but *'Jets'* features one that comes from out of nowhere. The album takes a turn on *'We've Got A File on You'*, going completely punk for a minute before going back to the layered art rock. The band

> **"Those who know the band from 'Song 2' or 'Parklife' may be thrown off by what they hear"**

Track List

SIDE A
Track 1: Ambulance
Track 2: Out Of Time
Track 3: Crazy Beat
SIDE B
Track 1: Good Song
Track 2: On The Way To The Club
Track 3: Brothers And Sisters
SIDE C
Track 1: Caravan
Track 2: We've Got A File On You
Track 3: Moroccan Peoples Revolutionary Bowls Club
SIDE D
Track 1: Jets
Track 2: Gene By Gene
Track 3: Battery In Your Leg

For *Think Tank* the band explored new culture and new recording methods

would use a lot of odd noises throughout the album such as jumping on a caravan at a farm to record samples of it squeaking. That's the kind of album you're getting.

The band recorded demos for *Think Tank* in 2001 at Damon Albarn's 13 studio in London but the Iraq war was on the horizon and Albarn, being an active pacifist chose along with the band to get away from the politics. This led the band along with their producer Ben Hillier to move to Marrakech in Morocco. While in a new country exploring a foreign culture, they decided to explore different recording methods so instead of recording in a big studio, they decided to set up the equipment in a barn and they would record while outside.

Norman Cook, or as he's better known as, Fatboy Slim produced the tracks *'Crazy Beat'* and *'Gene By Gene'*. His influence as well as Albarn's work from Gorillaz can clearly be heard on the prior with the electronic and dance rock feel. The album sleeve features one of the few commercially released pieces of artwork by graffiti artist Banksy, his pieces are featured on the back, front and inside on the gatefold. An original pressing of *Think Tank* can sell for a lot, although there are newer pressing that sell for significantly less.

Coxon left the band, but can be heard on *'Battery In Your Leg'*

Parklife (1994)

The album goes through a number of musical genres defined in Britain from punk to new-wave and somehow Blur would define a new one in Britpop with this album along with its singles *'Boys & Girls'* and *'Parklife'*.

13 (1999)

Britpop was on its way out and Blur decided to move on rather than try to milk what was left. *13* experimented with electronic sounds, darker themes and would lay the groundwork that they would expand on with *Think Tank*.

The Magic Whip (2015)

Blur are still experimenting by taking inspiration from different countries and expanding their sound, this time their muse was Asia. For their sound they mixed indie rock with dreamy textures, synth drums and other effects.

Elephant

White Stripes

Release Date: 2003 | **Record Label:** XL Recordings

Any rock band performs best when it remembers to take care of two important things. The first is to have a thought-out art direction; the second is to write songs that are simple, super-hooky and that the postman can whistle as he walks up your path.

The Detroit guitar/drums duo White Stripes had both of these essential features of a successful rock career totally in the bag when its fourth album, *Elephant*, was released in 2003. Sure, the red-and-white colour scheme promoted by Jack White and his ex-wife, Meg White, seems a little cheesy 14 years later, because we have all seen it so many times now, but the songs remain incredibly potent.

We're talking, of course, about *'Seven Nation*

Army', essentially a repeated guitar riff — alternately played in the guitar's natural frequency range and then downtuned in order to sound like a bass — and the infectious chorus that accompanies it. It's true that the White Stripes had built a fanbase before the release of *Elephant*, thanks to its aggressively focused take on old Nashville-style blues, recorded with vintage equipment, but it wasn't until the success of *'Seven Nation Army'* that the duo truly transcended its blues roots and became a chart-rock band.

Additional interest was stirred up by the fact that the group made a full-band sound even though there were only two of them, establishing a template directly responsible for the current success of duos such as Royal Blood, whose singer Mike Kerr recently said: "*'Seven Nation Army'* by the White Stripes could literally be the first thing you might teach someone to play, yet it's one of the most iconic riffs of our generation. It's international and it's sung in stadiums all round the world."

'Seven Nation Army' was followed by *'I Just Don't Know What To Do With Myself'*, *'The Hardest Button To Button'* and *'There's No Home For You Here'*, making *Elephant* an inescapable force from 2003 to 2005. The White Stripes' success assured, it continued as a recording and touring band until 2011, quitting with its legacy well intact.

Married couple Jack and Meg White formed the White Stripes duo in 1997

Track List

SIDE A
Track 1: Seven Nation Army
Track 2: Black Math
Track 3: There's No Home For You Here

SIDE B
Track 1: I Just Don't Know What To Do With Myself
Track 2: In The Cold, Cold Night
Track 3: I Want To Be The Boy To Warm Your Mother's Heart

SIDE C
Track 1: You've Got Her In Your Pocket
Track 2: Ball And Biscuit
Track 3: The Hardest Button To Button
Track 4: Little Acorns

SIDE D
Track 1: Hypnotize
Track 2: The Air Near My Fingers
Track 3: Girl, You Have No Faith In Medicine
Track 4: Well It's True That We Love One Another
Track 5: Who's To Say (Japan Only)
Track 6: Good To Me (Japan Only)

Madvillainy

Madvillain

Release Date: 2004 | **Record Label:** Stones Throw

The brainchild of rapper Daniel Dumile (aka MF Doom) and producer/DJ Otis Jackson Jr (whose stage name is Madlib), Madvillain has been sporadically active since this excellent debut album was released in 2004. This is at least partly responsible for the enigmatic image of both the duo and the album itself, which was so full of brilliant songs that a cult fanbase has grown up around it. Occasional hints that a full-blown sequel will be released have been dropped here and there, and only boost the legendary status of the music.

And believe us, the reputation of *Madvillainy* is wholly deserved. The rapping delivered by Dumile across the album — a sprawling double LP of multilayered samples and grooves from the old Public Enemy school — is forceful without ever being forced. Jackson's sound manipulation and focus on mellow textures makes the record a sonic pleasure: lush, widescreen and ambitious. Although there are plenty of observations from Dumile on the staple topics of hip hop — see *'America's Most Blunted'* for a thesis on the immortal herb, for example — the album doesn't generally venture into clichéd territory.

Most double albums suffer somewhat from a lack of variation across their four sides, making it rather difficult for the listener to keep paying attention after a certain number of songs. However, *Madvillainy* circumvents this issue by covering a phenomenal amount of ground, retaining certain essential tropes, such as tarmac-weakening bass frequencies. The duo brings in Indian orchestras, classic funk and soul samples from the Dr Dre-approved gene pool, and a whole raft of crazy extra layers, such as mad laughter and female choirs.

The overall feel is one of stoned benevolence: there's very little of the guns-and-gangs feel that typified American hip-hop of the previous decade, particularly from the West Coast. There's too much inventive sample-mining for that, and a sense of intelligence in the rhymes and accompaniment that is still a rarity in mainstream hip-hop — but which has always flourished in alternative urban music such as this.

Madvillainy was praised for its unique approach

Track List

SIDE A
Track 1: The Illest Villains
Track 2: Accordion
Track 3: Meat Grinder
Track 4: Bistro
Track 5: Raid

SIDE B
Track 1: America's Most Blunted
Track 2: Sickfit
Track 3: Rainbows
Track 4: Curls
Track 5: Do Not Fire!
Track 6: Money Folder

SIDE C
Track 1: Scene Two
Track 2: Shadows of Tomorrow
Track 3: Operation Lifesaver a.k.a. Mint Test
Track 4: Figaro
Track 5: Hardcore Hustle
Track 6: Strange Ways

SIDE D
Track 1: Intro
Track 2: Fancy Clown
Track 3: Eye
Track 4: Supervillain Theme
Track 5: All Caps
Track 6: Great Day
Track 7: Rhinestone Cowboy

Illinois

Sufjan Stevens

Release Date: 2005 | **Record Label:** Asthmatic Kitty/Secretly Canadian/Rough Trade

Some excitement was inevitably felt among followers of indie songwriter Sufjan Stevens when he announced in 2003 that his third album, *Michigan*, would be the first of a sequence of 50 that were devoted to all of the individual states of the United States of America. The album certainly sold well, but two albums later, *Illinois* — sometimes referred to as Illinoise or even *Sufjan Stevens Invites You To: Come On Feel The Illinoise*, because of its cover design — did even better than expected. It remains his bestselling work, which made his later admission that the 50-albums idea was merely a 'gimmick' only a little deflating.

Still, the album stands up perfectly well, unsupported by a concept other than its own, which was that the songs are inspired by the Midwestern state by which the album is titled. The first song that most people heard from the album, *'Casimir Pulaski Day'*, was a heartbreaking acoustic ballad in which Stevens told the tale of a personal bereavement — but good as it was, it didn't bear much resemblance to the rest of the album. Instead, Stevens was keener on piano textures, overblown strings and other exaggerated orchestral flourishes.

Stevens' interest in a wide range of subjects certainly matches the variety his musical scope. One of the sweeter songs deals with the mass murderer John Wayne Gacy Jr, while *'Chicago'* is a full-leaded rock anthem. On the second cut, the 53-word title beginning *'The Black Hawk War...'* takes as long to read as its running time, in which a huge plethora of instruments announces a solemn chord sequence. It is often highly ambitious music that hits its target expertly.

Illinois topped the Billboard Heatseekers chart on its release, which really was quite an achievement for music that was this obscure at the time. Stevens has remained a highly prolific recording artist since then, issuing a sequence of releases that continue to explore his personal, religious and political beliefs. The cynics among us who maintain the belief that the best pop, rock and even folk music is long in the past would do well to investigate this unusual musician's even more unusual work before simply passing it off as another attempt to leave their mark on music.

Track List

SIDE A
Track 1: Concerning The UFO Sighting Near Highland, Illinois
Track 2: The Black Hawk War
Track 3: Come On! Feel The Illinoise!
Track 4: John Wayne Gacy, Jr
Track 5: Jacksonville
Track 6: A Short Reprise For Mary Todd, Who Went Insane, But For Very Good Reasons

SIDE B
Track 1: Decatur, Or, Round Of Applause For Your Stepmother!
Track 2: One Last 'Whoo-Hoo!' For The Pullman!!
Track 3: Go! Chicago! Go! Yeah!
Track 4: Casimir Pulaski Day
Track 5: To The Workers Of The Rock River Valley Region

SIDE C
Track 1: The Man Of Metropolis Steals Our Hearts
Track 2: Prairie Fire That Wanders About (Peoria)
Track 3: A Conjunction Of Drones Simulating
Track 4: The Predatory Wasp Of The Palisades Is Out To Get Us!
Track 5: They Are Night Zombies!!
Track 6: Let's Hear That String Part Again
Track 7: In This Temple As In The Hearts Of Man For Whom He Saved The Earth

SIDE D
Track 1: The Seer's Tower
Track 2: The Tallest Man, The Broadest Shoulders
Track 3: Riffs And Variations
Track 4: Out Of Egypt, Into The Great Laugh Of Mankind
Track 5: The Avalanche

Fleet Foxes

Fleet Foxes

Release Date: 2008 | Record Label: Bella Union/Sub Pop

Many critics ranked Fleet Foxes as one of the best albums of 2008

Buy the Seattle band Fleet Foxes' first, self-titled album as the double LP reissue if you can, as it also includes its second EP, *Sun Giant*. Furthermore, the famous warmth inherent in vinyl albums' sound lends itself perfectly to the band's style — a layered, rich blend of close-harmony vocals, echoed soundscapes and subtle guitar tones.

Not bad for a debut album made by relatively inexperienced musicians. Fleet Foxes — initially singer Robin Pecknold and guitarist Skyler Skjelset — made no secret from the outset of its career of its admiration for classic American folk-rock acts, such as Neil Young and Crosby, Stills & Nash. Those artists' expert vocal arrangements and large-scale

instrumentation permeate Fleet Foxes' first album, along with a definite nod towards the eclecticism of British folk institutions, such as Fairport Convention. *'Ragged Wood'* is a great example of the former — there's an audible echo of CSN in the opening chant of *"Whoo-aah"* — while *'White Winter Hymnal'* has that old English sound expertly down.

It's not all nostalgic '60s worship around Fleet Foxes' house, though. Chiming electric guitars straight from the rock canon can be heard in songs such as *'He Doesn't Know Why'*, where the band reveals its understanding of stadium-sized songwriting. Little wonder it was discovered at super-hip festivals such as South by Southwest and Sasquatch! before making an impact overseas, notably in the UK. On this side of the pond, we've always been partial to a bit of American roots music (see also: Kings Of Leon) and close-harmony bands liberally equipped with facial hair, and so it proved with Fleet Foxes.

In the decade since the release of *Fleet Foxes*, the band has released a series of popular albums in the vein of the first one; its recipe has been enduringly popular, combining enough riff swagger to motivate arena audiences, while retaining the mellow folkie touches. How many other bands could incorporate layers of flute into a rock song and find itself welcomed by venues full of fans?

Track List

SIDE A
Track 1: Sun It Rises
Track 2: White Winter Hymnal
Track 3: Ragged Wood
Track 4: Tiger Mountain Peasant Song
Track 5: Quiet House
Track 6: He Doesn't Know Why

SIDE B
Track 1: Heard Them Stirring
Track 2: Your Protecto
Track 3: Meadowlarks
Track 4: Blue Ridge Mountains
Track 5: Oliver Jamesver a.k.a Mint Test

Neon Bible

Arcade Fire

Release Date: 2007 | **Record Label:** Merge Records

There's definitely something messianic, or at least religious, in the feel and themes of *Neon Bible*, the second album from Montreal's Arcade Fire. Canadians tend to have an individual take on rock music anyway, blending the bombast of American guitar music with the quirks and humour of British pop, and that's exactly how *Neon Bible* sounds, with its mixture of sideways philosophy and classic wall-of-sound songwriting dynamics. No wonder it bagged its creators over 400,000 sales, rave reviews and enviably high chart positions.

Appropriately, the album was recorded in an old church in rural Québec, purchased and converted into a studio by the band. Perhaps the recording environment lent itself to an introspective vibe, but the songs certainly dig deep into the psyche; singer Win Butler explored themes that seemed both abstract and relevant (*"Who here among us still believes in choice?"*) and the music often ventured into atmospheric Americana.

Piano, often treated with sinister echoes, ethereal backing vocals, a droned bass and layers of synth and strings also gave the music a cinematic feel. Splendidly, a massive church organ — or at least, a convincingly synthesised version of one — introduced and underpinned one of the album's best songs, *'Intervention'*. The same sense of presence and weight infuses *'No Cars Go'*, a studio-crafted thing of beauty featuring strata of brass and guitars which features a memorable harmony vocal.

All this chin-stroking seriousness aside, there was still a sense of fun on *Neon Bible*. *'The Well And The Lighthouse'* was an uptempo guitar anthem with the patented Joy Division-style bass-line that is the hallmark of so much indie rock, and while Butler's strained vocals occasionally become wearing, there's no denying the passion with which he delivers the song. See also (*'Antichrist Television Blues'*), a knowingly Bruce Springsteen-esque protest tune that builds and builds for the perfect stadium vibe.

As with many new — or at least new-ish — bands, Arcade Fire have lots to say and the means to say it in many different ways. Alongside the big

> **"Appropriately, the album was recorded in an old church in rural Québec..."**

Track List

SIDE A
Track 1: Black Mirror
Track 2: Keep The Car Running
Track 3: Neon Bible
Track 4: Intervention

SIDE B
Track 1: Black Wave/Bad Vibrations
Track 2: Ocean Of Noise
Track 3: The Well And The Lighthouse
Track 4: (Antichrist Television Blues)

SIDE C
Track 1: Windowsill
Track 2: No Cars Go
Track 3: My Body Is A Cage

dynamics of the more upfront songs, the band also take the intensity levels right back for moments of subtle charm. *'My Body Is A Cage'* is one of these, a spaced-out song featuring that amazing church organ again and an angelic choir straight from the classic movie-soundtrack genre. It doesn't stay in downbeat territory for long, though. Listen out for the moment at 2:20 when that organ and what sounds like hundreds of singers burst into action, underpinned by drums from hell.

Where Arcade Fire excel as composers is in their awareness of songwriting economy. Why change a key or chord gratuitously when a simple drone is more effective? Like U2, who the band supported after the album's release, Butler and his team are masters of allowing a bass-line to evolve beneath long, drawn-out keyboard and guitar notes. See *'Keep The Car Running'*, where these features are prominent, as well as the neat trick of letting a vocal whoop carry the chorus melody without needing to amend the instrumentation. The title track itself is

a persuasive song, without ever expanding beyond the paramaters of a slightly sinister ballad. Intoned rather than sung vocals keep the atmospherics intact, and the song fades away not long after it has begun — leaving a question mark answered by the more epic songs. On completing the album the listener is left with a satisfying feeling that Arcade Fire raise more questions than answers. What is spirituality? What is America? And where do the two meet?

Despite the sheer weightiness of the album's themes, *Neon Bible* found a huge and loyal audience, continuing Arcade Fire's ascent. The group had been on the way up since their debut album, Funeral, released three years earlier, but *Neon Bible* accelerated that progress. Today they're one of the biggest bands to emerge in the twilight years of the music industry, having sold enough albums to make a comfortable living before streaming and filesharing removed that career option.

OTHER ALBUMS

Funeral (2014)
Debuting with this collection of songs inspired by the deaths of several loved ones during its recording, Arcade Fire were walking a path of their very own. A flurry of industry awards greeted the album, and the band were on their way...

The Suburbs (2010)
Released in the wake of *Neon Bible*, *The Suburbs* debuted at the top of the charts in the UK, the US, Canada and Ireland. That's pretty fast progress for a band on its third album. David Byrne, sometime of Talking Heads, was a notable guest.

Reflektor (2013)
For album number four, they went large — recording a double LP, investigating the Haitian roots of the band in both its music and marketing, and exploring a wide range of cultural influences through its songwriting.

2010 ONWARDS...

My Beautiful Dark Twisted Fantasy

Kanye West

Release Date: 2010 | Record Label: Roc-A-Fella/Def Jam

What do you do when you hit rock bottom? When a stress and ego-fuelled outburst makes you a target for every tabloid in the western hemisphere? When the biggest tour of your career to date falls apart in the aftermath? When the president is on record calling you an asshole? If you're Kanye West, you fly to Hawaii, you take some time off, and then you get to work.

What happened over the course of that Hawaiian exile in 2009-10 was akin to a hip-hop version of the Avengers assembling. Word was put out and, over the following weeks and months, a steady stream of artists jetted out a sprawling recording complex on Oahu. The anecdotes from those sessions paint a vivid picture: Kanye eagerly flicking through photos of nude models with Nicki Minaj; Kid Cudi and RZA working out in the gym while Ye and co shoot hoops with the locals; Bon Iver's Justin Vernon rolling joints with Rick Ross during a break from recording. Kanye

> **"Among all of the organised chaos an album started to come together"**

barely slept, taking infrequent naps at the studio, but among all this organised chaos an album started to come together. For a while it was known simply as 'Good Ass Job' but, ever the showman, he eventually settled on something with a touch more pizzazz: *My Beautiful Dark Twisted Fantasy*.

Kanye has always been an MC in the truest sense. He assembles, curates and collaborates. His albums are events, and Twisted Fantasy is the grandest of them all; a musical Met Gala whose guest list is a who's who of industry glitterati (and Cyhi Da Prynce). But while the feature-fest album has become a risible staple of mainstream hip-hop (our regards to DJ Khaled), the contributions here are essential, cherry-picked and refined by West and his team. Speaking to Complex, producer Q-Tip described the process: "You see how he integrates and transforms everyone's contributions... What he does is alchemy, really."

With so many ingredients in play, it's easy to imagine an album that groans under the weight of its

Track List

SIDE A
Track 1:	Dark Fantasy
Track 2:	Gorgeous
Track 3:	Power
Track 4:	David Bowie — Moonage Daydream
Track 5:	All Of The Lights
Track 6:	Monster

SIDE B
Track 1:	So Appalled
Track 2:	Devil In A New Dress
Track 3:	Runaway
Track 4:	Hell Of A Life
Track 5:	Blame Game
Track 6:	Lost In The World
Track 7:	Who Will Survive In America

In what might be one of his most impressive feats to date, he headlined Glastonbury in 2015

guitar samples set the stage for Rick Ross' delectable cameo, a series of booming boasts that culminates in him "making love to the angel of death." Even by Rozay's standards, it's spectacularly over-the-top. Elsewhere, a sneering Pusha T helps toast to the douchebags on *'Runaway'*, John Legend (and an outrageous Chris Rock) talk love/hate relationships on *'Blame Game'*, and on *'Monster'*, Nicki Minaj goes from Young Money crew member to burgeoning rap icon in the space of one blistering, persona-switching verse.

As a package, *Twisted Fantasy* is suitably extravagant, the sleeve all crimson and gold with a striking border framing one of George Condo's five surreal pieces of artwork — which range from nightmarish portraits to toasting ballerinas. And next to the jewel-case minimalism of *Yeezus* and the multimedia melange that is *The Life Of Pablo*, *MBDTF* feels especially lavish. It's still Kanye's most unabashedly opulent album, and as the years go by it seems increasingly unlikely that he'll make another record like it.

And if he doesn't, then that's okay. The album speaks for itself, albeit through many voices. Kanye has neither the first nor the last word — those fall to Minaj and the late Gil Scott-Heron respectively — but he doesn't need to. This is *his* show, *his* magnum opus, *his* beautiful, dark, twisted fantasy.

credits list. The reality is anything but. For one thing, Kanye's rapping is as good as it's ever been — early highlights *'Gorgeous'* and *'Power'* both feature career-high bars, before Elton John's brief piano interlude leads into the cacophonous, star-studded banger, *'All Of The Lights'*. Around those verses, that aforementioned alchemy is evident. Kanye gets the best out of his collaborators, both on the mic and behind the glass, letting each of them steal the limelight momentarily while never receding into the background himself.

On *'Devil In A New Dress'*, layers of decadent

After returning from recording *Twisted Fantasy*, Kanye entered into a kind of resurgence

Dimitrios Kambouris/Getty Images

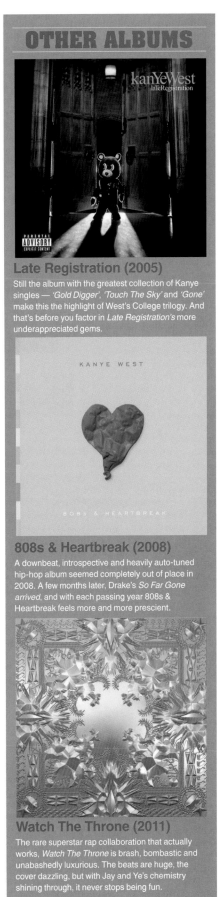

OTHER ALBUMS

Late Registration (2005)
Still the album with the greatest collection of Kanye singles — *'Gold Digger'*, *'Touch The Sky'* and *'Gone'* make this the highlight of West's College trilogy. And that's before you factor in *Late Registration's* more underappreciated gems.

808s & Heartbreak (2008)
A downbeat, introspective and heavily auto-tuned hip-hop album seemed completely out of place in 2008. A few months later, Drake's *So Far Gone* arrived, and with each passing year 808s & Heartbreak feels more and more prescient.

Watch The Throne (2011)
The rare superstar rap collaboration that actually works, *Watch The Throne* is brash, bombastic and unabashedly luxurious. The beats are huge, the cover dazzling, but with Jay and Ye's chemistry shining through, it never stops being fun.

Have One On Me

Joanna Newsom

Release Date: 2010 | **Record Label:** Drag City

It's a miracle that Joanna Newsom is so successful that only three albums in to her career, her label allowed her to issue a triple album. It's also a miracle that people bought it in large numbers, and that those same people had the time and the patience to absorb it. So much for the ADHD generation, and so much for the often-stated 'death of pop music'.

Newsom's music, a wilfully unusual combination of harp and vocal songs with unusual instrumentation, is often beautiful, but it isn't remotely commercial, while her voice — a breathy, affected lisp from the Kate Bush school — should by rights have no place in the age of walrus-lunged R&B divas. And yet here the album is: six widely acclaimed sides of vinyl that attracted many a positive nod from critics. They didn't all like it, of course — that would be impossible — but if Have One on Me had been released in 1990 or 2000 instead of 2010, it would have been widely dismissed as pretentious, overblown nonsense, and given a critical kicking on its way to the bargain bin. Times have indeed changed.

Highlight choices from the 18 songs here are obviously arbitrary, but you could do worse than starting with 'Good Intentions Paving Company', a soulful piano ballad that channelled all of Newsom's Bush and Tori Amos influences into a solid, melodic

chunk. 'You And Me, Bess' adds a jazz trumpet to the vibe, with a witch-like vocal atop a plucked ukulele, and the dynamics stripped right back for maximum impact. In fact, fully over-the-top arrangements are less prevalent on this album than they are on the albums Newsom has released before and since this one, with a sparse feel generally at the top of the mix.

So how did Joanna Newsom become so popular? It's a mystery, albeit a welcome one. She has found a willing audience of listeners in the UK and elsewhere, perhaps because music fans outside her native California are a little bit more open to unorthodox moods than elsewhere. Either way, the fact that a triple LP such as this could find such appreciation can only be a good sign.

Newsom on stage in 2005

Track List

SIDE A
Track 1: Easy
Track 2: Have One On Me
Track 3: '81
SIDE B
Track 1: Good Intentions Paving Company
Track 2: No Provenance
Track 3: Baby Birch
SIDE C
Track 1: On A Good Day
Track 2: You And Me, Bess
Track 3: In California
SIDE D
Track 1: Jackrabbits
Track 2: Go Long
Track 3: Occident
SIDE E
Track 1: Soft As Chalk
Track 2: Esme
Track 3: Autumn
SIDE F
Track 1: Ribbon Bows
Track 2: Kingfisher
Track 3: Does Not Suffice

Bon Iver

Bon Iver

Release Date: 2011 | **Record Label:** Jagjaguwar/4AD

The Bon Iver origin story is the stuff of indie-folk legend. Depressed, disillusioned, creatively and emotionally exhausted, Justin Vernon left his band and his relationship, and drove to rural Wisconsin. There, he holed himself up in a hunting cabin for months and made a haunting, deeply personal record that, against all odds, became a huge hit.

For Emma, Forever Ago remains a singularly beautiful album, but *Bon Iver's* eponymous follow-up takes its predecessor's introverted perspective and turns it outward. It's grander in scope, variety and ambition; no longer is this the sound of one man and his guitar alone in the woods.

In terms of sheer range of instrumentation, Bon Iver marks a significant departure from the band's debut. Synths meld with horns, violins and electric guitars across the ten tracks, with Vernon's distinctive falsetto the thread that weaves through the record's musical road trip. The percussion also really stands out in the album. From the military drumroll on opening track *'Perth'* to the rock stomp that propels *'Calgary'*, there's a rhythm, a sort of pulse that was absent from *For Emma's* quiet, gossamer songs. *'Holocene'* captures the very best of both these styles; a simple guitar melody is joined by Vernon's soaring vocals, which slowly build to a cathartic climax: *"And*

at once I knew, I was not magnificent."

Bon Iver's layered, vibrant sound is mirrored in its cover artwork. Gregory Euclide's piece is a surreal tapestry of tranquil lakes, remote homesteads and woodland clearings. The vignettes blur and overlap, creating a dreamlike landscape that perfectly captures the album's sonic sense of place. It's one of the most beautiful sleeves you'll find anywhere.

The same can certainly be said for Bon Iver as a whole. Vernon's second album is a triumph; warm and lush and full of moments of unadulterated joy, just like the jangly guitars of *'Towers'*, and the kitschy keyboard riff of '80s soft-rock closer *'Beth/Rest'*. After the winter blues of *For Emma*, it's somewhat of a thawing; spring, pressed to vinyl.

Track List

SIDE A
Track 1: Perth
Track 2: Minnesota, WI
Track 3: Holocene
Track 4: Towers
Track 5: Michicant
SIDE B
Track 1: Hinnom, TX
Track 2: Wash.
Track 3: Calgary
Track 4: Lisbon, OH
Track 5: Beth/Rest

Bon Iver live in Sydney, Australia

El Camino

The Black Keys

Release Date: 2011 | **Record Label:** Nonesuch

The success of the White Stripes in the '00s occasionally obscured the almost equally prestigious trajectory of the Black Keys in the same decade. The reasons for this were obvious: although the Stripes came from Detroit, Michigan and the Keys from Akron, Ohio, both bands were guitar-and-drums duos; both were obsessed with playing vintage-sounding, lo-fi blues rock with old gear and in veteran recording studios; both of the frontmen used effects to create both guitar and bass sounds with a single instrument; both were prone to sing in a falsetto as well as a blues wail; and (perhaps trivially) both bands had colours in their names. The two groups even clashed, later in their career, with threats exchanged on Twitter, although a reconciliation was apparently reached.

Those admittedly convincing similarities aside, the Black Keys have a catalogue of their own which is just as appealing as that of Jack and Meg White. They also deserve widespread respect for the many years they spent — from their formation in 2002 until

they broke big around eight years later — on the road, driving themselves from gig to gig in their own van (the 'Gray Ghost', as it was nicknamed) with almost no money to support the tour. A few months of that lifestyle is enough to drive most bands to a premature split; eight years and counting of the classically brutal no-sleep, no-food slog requires superhuman endurance. But singer Dan Auerbach and drummer Pat Carney did it, and made it work.

The point at which we join the Black Keys' story is in 2011, on the release of their seventh album El Camino, which translates as 'the way' or 'the path' from Spanish. Thanks to the success of the duo's 2010 album Brothers, some long-awaited income was coming their way at last, and rather than sit back and enjoy a well-earned break, Auerbach and Carney plunged straight into a new record. Between the album itself and the opening cut, 'Lonely Boy', the Black Keys won three Grammy awards, and it's easy to see why. Blessed with a decent recording budget and a skilled producer in Brian 'Danger Mouse' Burton, the album contains a suite of appealing, catchy songs

> **"A few months of that lifestyle is enough to drive most bands to a premature split"**

Track List

SIDE A
Track 1:	Lonely Boy
Track 2:	Dead And Gone
Track 3:	Gold On The Ceiling
Track 4:	Little Black Submarines
Track 5:	Money Maker

SIDE B
Track 1:	Run Right Back
Track 2:	7 Sister
Track 3:	Hell Of A Season
Track 4:	Stop Stop
Track 5:	Nova Baby
Track 6:	Mind Eraser

The success of The Black Keys often seemed over shadowed by The White Stripes

that are blues-indebted rather than being straight blues. Indie influences can be heard in the choppy guitar lines, and a billowy bass sound keeps the groove locked in tightly on songs such as Sister, a subtle but compelling guitar workout.

El Camino was acclaimed for its inclusion of different musical influences to those which had permeated the Black Keys' previous work. Most notably, a glam-rock feel straight from the T-Rex and Sweet school was all over songs such as *'Run Right Back'*, a stomping moshpit anthem with simplicity its main focus. Later, the album peaked with *'Hell Of A Season'*, based on a driving bass-line that was two parts Clash and another part Kings Of Leon. Fans of the headbanging persuasion, meanwhile, were treated to *'Money Maker'*, a riff-storm straight out of the heavy-rock canon of the '70s.

Another high point is *'Little Black Submarines'*, an acoustic ballad which builds to the full Zeppelin-style Sturm und Drang, while *'Hell Of A Season'* is stripped-down to the bone for a feel that is quirky and danceable, while staying close to the Keys' vintage roots. As for the album-closer, *'Mind Eraser'*, it's a slick piece of radio-rock with a persistent guitar motif that offers an ending to the record that is neither up- or downbeat. There was so much on this album to enjoy that it's little wonder it was a widespread success.

The overall impression is one of a band which is entirely at ease with its method after many years of experience — and which, unusually, still has something to say. This also goes for the accompanying videos, one of which, *'Gold On The Ceiling'*, features the two men carried in baby carriers by giant versions of themselves. That's thinking outside the box for you.

The Black Keys spent years driving themselves around from gig to gig

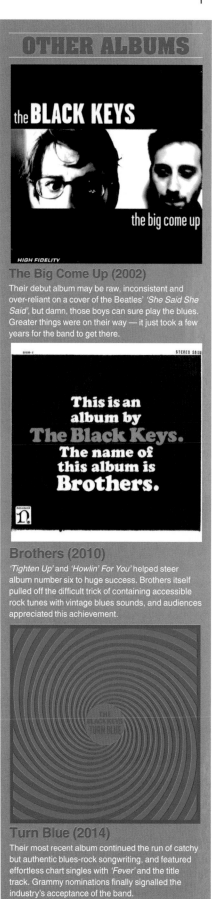

OTHER ALBUMS

The Big Come Up (2002)
Their debut album may be raw, inconsistent and over-reliant on a cover of the Beatles' *'She Said She Said'*, but damn, those boys can sure play the blues. Greater things were on their way — it just took a few years for the band to get there.

Brothers (2010)
'Tighten Up' and *'Howlin' For You'* helped steer album number six to huge success. Brothers itself pulled off the difficult trick of containing accessible rock tunes with vintage blues sounds, and audiences appreciated this achievement.

Turn Blue (2014)
Their most recent album continued the run of catchy but authentic blues-rock songwriting, and featured effortless chart singles with *'Fever'* and the title track. Grammy nominations finally signalled the industry's acceptance of the band.

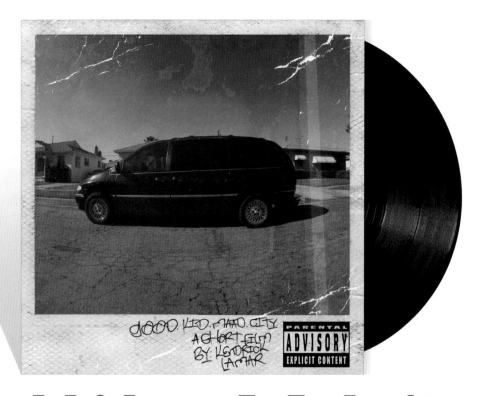

good kid, m.A.A.d city

Kendrick Lamar

Release Date: 2012 | **Record Label:** Top Dawg/Aftermath/Interscope

It wasn't without warning. There had been half a dozen mixtapes, numerous features and several high-profile co-signs in the lead up to Kendrick Lamar's major label debut. There had also been an excellent, independently released album in *Section.80*. But though these harbingers hinted at a prodigious talent from hip hop's most fertile West Coast hotbed, they didn't fully prepare us for *good kid, m.A.A.d city (GKMC)*.

Across more than an hour of riveting rhymes, sweeping production and brutally compelling storytelling, Kendrick takes a melting pot of influences and rolls them into one mesmerising chronicle of Compton life. In doing so, he assumes the mantle of the city's great hope; a point made explicit on the Dr Dre-featuring closer, *'Compton'*.

But though it acknowledges its heritage, *GKMC* is a long way from the furious gangsta rap of N.W.A, or *The Chronic's* synth-fuelled G-funk. The scenes from Kendrick's life — and the lives of countless other youths — are described in vivid, meticulous detail: freezing at the sight of *"Two n****s, two black hoodies"* (*'Sherane'*); swerving to evade police after a robbery (*'The Art Of Peer Pressure'*); foaming at the mouth after smoking a blunt laced with cocaine (*'m.A.A.d city'*).

You'll find poetry intermingled with these uncompromising portraits, however. Kendrick is certainly more soulful and lyrically abstract on *'Bitch, Don't Kill My Vibe'*; he's also more wistful and contemplative on *'Money Trees'*, the woozy beat framing reflections on morality and mortality in the hood: *"Everybody gon' respect the shooter/But the one in front of the gun lives forever."*

Kendrick Lamar performs on the Coachella Stage

Track List

SIDE A
Track 1: Sherane a.k.a. Master Splinter's Daughter
Track 2: Bitch, Don't Kill My Vibe
Track 3: Backseat Freestyle
Track 4: The Art Of Peer Pressure
Track 5: Money Trees
Track 6: Poetic Justice
SIDE B
Track 1: good kid
Track 2: m.A.A.d city
Track 3: Swimming Pools (Drank)
Track 4: Sing About Me, I'm Dying Of Thirst
Track 5: Real
Track 6: Compton

Kevin Winter/Getty Images

These are themes and ideas that recur throughout Kendrick's work, but on *good kid, m.A.A.d city* they're realised with striking clarity — that it's billed on the sleeve as 'A short film' speaks to that. It's by no means a party record — though throw on *'Backseat Freestyle'* or *'Swimming Pools'* and you could mistake it for one — but neither is it overwhelming. And with each listen, new insights and moments of genius reveal themselves in Kendrick's swirling narrative.

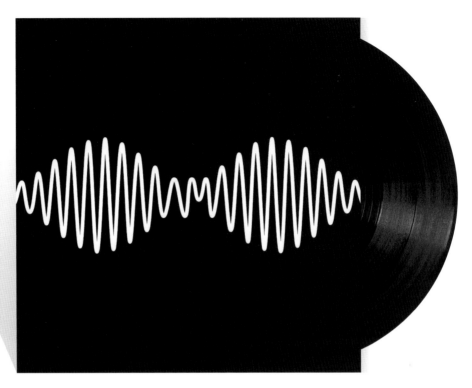

AM

Arctic Monkeys

Release Date: 2013 | **Record Label:** Domino

Drop the needle on AM and the first thing you'll hear is the hypnotic thump of Matt Helders' drums. A wake-up call that gives you five seconds to brace for Jamie Cook's titanic, swaggering guitar to make its entrance on *'Do I Wanna Know?'*. This is the first

Arctic Monkeys performs at the Golden Gate Park on 8 August 2014 in San Francisco, California

huge riff to rear its head on Arctic Monkeys' fifth, and most electric album, but it's far from the last.

Across 12 lean tracks, the four-piece reel off a selection of foot-stomping anthems, funk-infused earworms, and a couple of simmering ballads for good measure. Frontman Alex Turner's distinctive vocals straddle these styles with ease, switching from an invigorating howl to a languid croon as the occasion demands. But while his charismatic delivery is front and centre, the other elements of *AM* feel just as taut; the music more confident and cohesive than it's sounded before.

In this way, *AM* marks a sort of conclusion to the second act of the Arctic Monkeys' career. The hyperactive indie post-punk of the band's first pair of albums seems a long way off, and the heavier, more experimental sound that began with the release of 2009's *Humbug* is honed and explored much further here. Turner, in particular, embraces his transformation from sharp, Sheffield-born smartarse to the swaggering full-blown rock star we see on stage today. Along the way, some of the edges have been filed from his signature South Yorkshire drawl, but that's not to say it's been sanitised, and in the meantime his stylistic range has expanded to complement his songwriting versatility.

With that in mind, *AM* is a perfect demonstration

of the extent of the band's repertoire. *'Do I Wanna Know?'* and *'R U Mine?'* are straight-up stadium-sized hits, and it's no surprise that AM coincided with Arctic Monkeys' second headline set at Glastonbury. But as on albums past, things peak when they slow down a little. Whether in the wistful sleaziness of *'No. 1 Party Anthem'* or the sultry sway of *'I Wanna Be Yours'*, it's between the strutting and preening that *AM* is at its most alluring, and that the band sounds really, truly at home.

Track List

SIDE A

Track 1: Do I Wanna Know?
Track 2: R U Mine?
Track 3: One For The Road
Track 4: Arabella
Track 5: I Want It All
Track 6: No. 1 Party Anthem

SIDE B

Track 1: Mad Sounds
Track 2: Fireside
Track 3: Why'd You Only Call Me When You're High?
Track 4: Snap Out Of It
Track 5: Knee Socks
Track 6: I Wanna Be Yours

Random Access Memories

Daft Punk

Release Date: 2013 | Record Label: Various/Columbia

Some might suggest that it was arrogant of Daft Punk to release its fourth album and not bother putting their name to it. The truth of the matter is though, is that they simply didn't need to. Thomas Bangalter and Manuel de Homem-Christo have been active as Daft Punk since 1993 and their distinctive robotic headgear is arguably as recognisable as their music. Indeed, many casual fans of the French duo will have never seen them outside of character, so it could be argued that Warren Fu's striking cover is the first album in the band's 24-year history to actually show their faces (from a certain point of view). Dig a little deeper though and you begin to realise that there's a lot of clever stuff being bandied about on that seemingly simple design. The jet black background, distinctive font and copious amounts of chrome mimic albums from the late '70s and early '80s, which perfectly matches the musical themes that the duo have looked to across the album's 13 tracks. It could also be argued that *Random Access Memories'* cover is a nod to the band's earlier 2001

single, *'Harder Better Faster Stronger'*, which featured a number of characters comprised of both human and android parts.

One other noticeable thing about *Random Access Memories* font and styling is that it's incredibly similar to Michael Jackson's *Thriller*. We'd argue that this is intentional on the pair's behalf as they mention the influence Jackson's music had on the creation of the album. The king of pop wasn't the only person the duo looked to for inspiration. The likes of The Eagles, The Doobie Brothers and Fleetwood Mac enabled the pair to create the 'west coast vibe' they desired. *Hotel California*, *Rumours* and Pink Floyd's *The Dark Side Of The Moon* would help mould the albums sound, but the pair also wanted the album to feel like a journey, citing examples such as The Beatles' *The White Album* and The Who's *Quadrophenia*. The ambition of *Random Access Memories* is best summed up by the exceptional *'Giorgio By Moroder'*, which features a monologue by the Italian musician Giorgio Moroder which effortlessly captures not only his own musical style, but also the eras of music he discusses.

> **"The striking cover is the first album in the band's 24-year history to show their faces"**

Track List

SIDE A
Track 1: Give Life Back To Music
Track 2: The Game Of Love
Track 3: Giorgio By Moroder

SIDE B
Track 1: Within
Track 2: Instant Crush
Track 3: Lost Yourself To Dance

SIDE C
Track 1: Touch
Track 2: Get Lucky
Track 3: Beyond

SIDE D
Track 1: Motherboard
Track 2: Fragments Of Time
Track 3: Doin' It Right
Track 4: Contact

Daft Punk attends the WSJ Magazine's 'Innovator Of The Year' Awards 2013 at The Museum of Modern Art on November 6, 2013 in New York City

Moroder wasn't the only musician Daft Punk collaborated with. Nile Rodgers appears on three of *Random Access Memories'* key songs, including the lead single *'Get Lucky'* and *'Lose Yourself To Dance'*, which both also feature Pharrell Williams. Other contributors include Julian Casablancas, Todd Edwards, Panda Bear DJ Falcon, Chilly Gonzales and Paul Williams, making *Random Access Memories* the most collaborative piece of work that Daft Punk has published. This collaboration with artists young and old creates an incredibly diverse sound that's quite like anything Daft Punk has done previously. Insanely ambitious — it was originally planned as a four-disc box set due to the sheer amount of content amassed — *Random Memory Access* is the perfect starting point for anyone wishing to discover a band at the height of its powers. It's unclear when Daft Punk's next album

will arrive (the pair have been relatively quiet aside from some collaborations with The Weeknd) but one thing is clear, when their fifth album does turn up it's going to have its work cut out.

Random Access Memories was released as vinyl was becoming fashionable again, so it's incredibly easy to get a brand new copy at a very reasonable price. If you do want to spend a small fortune on the album then go for the Limited Edition set, released in 2014 and restricted to 2,500 units. In addition to being presented in a cloth-bound box, the LP features exclusive gold and silver foil labels, there's an accompanying 56-page book of images from the album's recording sessions, as well as a 10' vinyl containing an interview with Giorgio Moroder. The lavish boxset contains numerous other goodies and sells for as much as £600, but it's an essential piece of Daft Punk lore.

Daft Punk performs at the Coachella Music Festival on 29 April 2006 in Indio, California

OTHER ALBUMS

Homework (1997)

Daft Punk's first album was a huge success, bringing French house music to the worldwide stage. It's fuelled by two huge singles, *'Da Funk'* and *'Around The World'* and has sold over 2 million copies.

Discovery (2001)

Discovery was another huge hit for Daft Punk and saw the duo adopt their robotic personas. The pair continued to invigorate the music scene and had their first collaboration with Todd Edwards.

Tron OST (2010)

A futuristic film needs a suitably futuristic soundtrack and Daft Punk's stunning score perfectly sets the tone of the movie. It's a beautifully crafted piece of work that's far better than the film it accompanies.

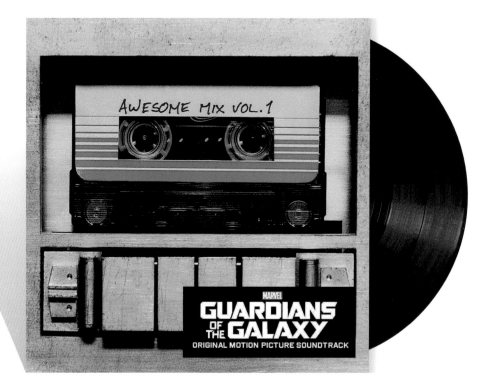

Guardians Of The Galaxy: Awesome Mix Vol. 1

Various Artists

Release Date: 2014 | Record Label: Hollywood Records

Compilation records are everywhere — see your local supermarket album chart for confirmation — and they are, more often than not, pretty **uninspiring.** Though the odd collection strikes gold, these albums are usually either too cheap — featuring a selection of songs that were available to license easily and inexpensively — or too safe — recycling the same few hits that you've heard a thousand times before.

The high-profile movie soundtrack has also made something of a resurgence in recent years, though not necessarily a welcome one. Frequently attached to blockbusters adapted from young adult fiction, these albums boast star-studded line-ups of artists and collaborators who conspire to make something that's generally little more than a collection of B-sides. So, when we tell you that a movie soundtrack that also happens to be a compilation album is one of the 100 vinyl records you should own, we'll forgive you for harbouring a little scepticism.

When *Guardians Of The Galaxy* arrived, however, it was different. A comic book oddity that was

somewhat bizarrely given the big-budget Marvel movie treatment, there were no iconic costume-sporting superheroes here. Instead, the film's motley crew of characters featured smugglers, assassins, an anthropomorphic raccoon, and a tree…creature. But here's the thing: *Guardians Of The Galaxy* might well be the best film Marvel's ever made.

While much of the credit for this goes to director James Gunn and the excellent ensemble cast, a huge part of what made the film so unexpectedly great was its soundtrack. Try naming a single musical moment from another Marvel film. Any luck? Unless you're a big fan of dull, generic blockbuster dirges then we're guessing not. This is partly by design; the studio has a style guide that its movies are encouraged to adhere to, for better or worse. But in Guardians, the soundtrack shackles came off. Standout musical moments are everywhere, thanks to its embrace of an eclectic mix of '70s and '80s pop.

There's the moody opening sequence that's brilliantly upended when Chris Pratt dons headphones and begins strutting to Redbone's *'Come And Get Your Love'. 'Cherry Bomb'* by The Runaways blares over a smirk-inducing montage as

Track List

SIDE A
Track 1: Blue Swede — Hooked On A Feeling
Track 2: Raspberries — Go All The Way
Track 3: Norman Greenbaum — Spirit In The Sky
Track 4: David Bowie — Moonage Daydream
Track 5: Elvin Bishop — Fooled Around And Fell In Love
Track 6: 10cc — I'm Not In Love

SIDE B
Track 1: The Jackson 5 — I Want You Back
Track 2: Redbone — Come And Get Your Love
Track 3: The Runaways — Cherry Bomb
Track 4: Rupert Holmes — Escape (The Piña Colada Song)
Track 5: Five Stairsteps — O-o-h Child
Track 6: Marvin Gaye And Tammi Terrell — Ain't No Mountain High Enough

"In the age of iTunes and Spotify... it's rarer to have that sort of authorship represented on vinyl"

the crew gear up for a climactic dogfight. *Guardians* even makes the tired post-credits scene worth waiting for by including a delightful dance sequence set to The Jackson 5's *'I Want You Back'*. And then there's *'Hooked On A Feeling'*, the film's unofficial theme song. With its 'ooga-chaka' intro and jaunty horns, it's the sort of goofy, bombastic tune that

captures *Guardians Of The Galaxy's* tone to a tee.

If you want to get meta, there's also a parallel between *Awesome Mix Vol. 1* the motion picture soundtrack, and *Awesome Mix Vol. 1* as it appears in the film. For Chris Pratt's Peter Quill, this tape, these songs, are a link to the past, but they're also a jumping off point for a whole universe of incredible music. It shouldn't be forgotten that many of the folks watching *Guardians* would have missed out on these songs the first time around. For those who want to revisit this golden era, there can be few better introductions.

Admittedly, there's something a little off about owning a self-styled mixtape on vinyl (the sleeve even sports a giant tape deck, just to hammer home the aesthetic). But there's also something particularly rewarding about listening to a perfectly curated record like this. In the age of iTunes and Spotify, making a playlist is a matter of a couple of clicks and a handful of drags, but it's rarer to have that sort of authorship represented on vinyl.

More dedicated collectors will most likely own some, or all, of the tracks here in one form or another, but *Awesome Mix Vol. 1* has already flipped through dozens of the '70s' greatest hits and its choices are impeccable. That's not to say it's an exhaustive 'best of the decade' record — not even close — but there's no chaff here, no B-sides or deep cuts, just a dozen brilliant, complementary hits, pure and simple. In a word, it's awesome.

Guardians **might as well not be a part of the Marvel Cinematic Universe, it's just that good**

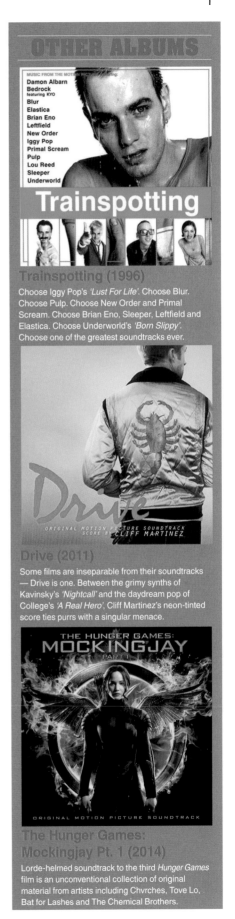

OTHER ALBUMS

MUSIC FROM THE MOTION PICTURE featuring:
Damon Albarn
Bedrock featuring KYO
Blur
Elastica
Brian Eno
Leftfield
New Order
Iggy Pop
Primal Scream
Pulp
Lou Reed
Sleeper
Underworld

Trainspotting

Trainspotting (1996)

Choose Iggy Pop's *'Lust For Life'*. Choose Blur. Choose Pulp. Choose New Order and Primal Scream. Choose Brian Eno, Sleeper, Leftfield and Elastica. Choose Underworld's *'Born Slippy'*. Choose one of the greatest soundtracks ever.

Drive (2011)

Some films are inseparable from their soundtracks — Drive is one. Between the grimy synths of Kavinsky's *'Nightcall'* and the daydream pop of College's *'A Real Hero'*, Cliff Martinez's neon-tinted score ties purrs with a singular menace.

The Hunger Games: Mockingjay Pt. 1 (2014)

Lorde-helmed soundtrack to the third *Hunger Games* film is an unconventional collection of original material from artists including Chvrches, Tove Lo, Bat for Lashes and The Chemical Brothers.

Lazaretto

Jack White

Release Date: 2014 | **Record Label:** Third Man/XL/Columbia

On his second solo record since The White Stripes disbanded in 2011, self-proclaimed vinyl junkie Jack White dug deep into his bag of tricks and created an all-singing, all-dancing marvel in wax. Released on White's own label, Third Man Records, *Lazaretto* is one of a rare breed — an album produced for the sole purpose of being enjoyed under a needle. White's songwriting and musicianship (though both exemplary as ever) play second fiddle to the plethora of innovative techniques that have been used in the record's production.

Pressed in seldom-used flat-edged 180g vinyl, audiophiles will be pleased to learn that absolutely zero compression was used during recording, mixing or mastering of the LP. Not only does the aptly dubbed 'Ultra LP' follow a different running order to the CD/digital release, but some alternate mixes were also exclusively used on the vinyl. The album is presented in a soft-touch, aqueous-coated jacket, while a die-cut poly-lined inner sleeve protects the disc.

The array of special features begin on Side A, which plays from the inside out and holds a first-of-its-kind hand-etched hologram of spinning angels in the dead wax at the centre of the disc. Each side conceals an untitled hidden track under the centre labels, one of which plays at 78rpm and the other at 45rpm, making

Lazaretto a three-speed record to boot.

Side B's opening track, *Just One Drink,* utilises dual-groove technology, which sees two grooves cut side-by-side, playing either the full intro to a song or an acoustic intro to the song, depending on where the needle is dropped. The grooves ultimately join for the body song. Each side of the record ends with locked grooves too, of which Side A's is believed to be the first on an LP's outside edge.

A US-only, limited-edition pressing on blue and white split-coloured vinyl was also released, which includes a bonus 7" (featuring two demo tracks from the album) and alternate cover art.

Jack White, Orlando Calling Music Festival, November 2011

Track List

SIDE A
Track 1: Three Women
Track 2: Lazaretto
Track 3: Temporary Ground
Track 4: Would You Fight For My Love?
Track 5: High Ball Stepper
SIDE B
Track 1: Just One Drink
Track 2: Alone In My Home
Track 3: That Black Bat Licorice
Track 4: Entitlement
Track 5: I Think I Found The Culprit
Track 6: Want And Able

The Epic

Kamasi Washington

Release Date: 2015 | **Record Label:** Brainfeeder

Any musician who releases a debut album called *The Epic* — and spreads it over six sides of vinyl — had better be prepared for a critical shoeing if said album falls short of perfection. It says much for jazz saxophonist Kamasi Washington, therefore, that not only did his first album attract unanimously positive scores, it transcended the jazz audience and became a must-buy for the mainstream. Name another triple album that has done the same? No, us neither.

If 'epic' was the flavour that Washington was aiming for with this expansive, ambitious recording, he achieved it alright. Lush orchestration, a huge variety of sound sources, and a band largely made up of young, hungry, avant-garde musicians combine on 17 songs that cover a wide range of emotions. Vocal tracks, instrumentals, sparse arrangements with only one or two instruments, fully worked-up barrages of sound… they're all here, and never predictably.

High points are many, depending on the listener's preference. For example, *'Henrietta Our Hero'* is a big-band behemoth that wouldn't sound out of place on the soundtrack of a '50s' Hollywood weepie. Washington's spiralling saxophone is at the heart of the music, of course, but he's no micromanaging bandleader, allowing his cast of musicians to explore their frequency space at leisure. Listen to *'Askim'*, a workout for the fingers of electric bassist Stephen *'Thundercat'* Bruner; or *'Cherokee'*, a drums and choir anthem that is equally a soul or R&B composition as much as a jazz tune.

The reason why *The Epic* matters is because, at the time of its release in 2015 as today, jazz is a dying art form, much as its fans prefer to deny it. The music hasn't been a truly powerful commercial force since 1975, and since then it has only been seriously significant in the form of jazz-rock. To hear an album that successfully nods to the '50s' cool jazz movement, and to see it perform well, is refreshing indeed.

The Epic successfully takes us back to the 1950s' jazz movement

Track List

SIDE A
Track 1:	Change Of The Guard
Track 2:	Isabelle
Track 3:	Final Thought

SIDE B
Track 1:	The Next Step
Track 2:	Askim

SIDE C
Track 1:	The Rhythm Changes
Track 2:	Leroy And Lanisha
Track 3:	Re Run

SIDE D
Track 1:	Miss Understanding
Track 2:	Henrietta Our Hero
Track 3:	Seven Prayers
Track 4:	Cherokee

SIDE E
Track 1:	The Magnificent 7
Track 2:	Re Run Home

SIDE F
Track 1:	Malcolm's Them
Track 2:	Clair De Lune
Track 3:	The Message